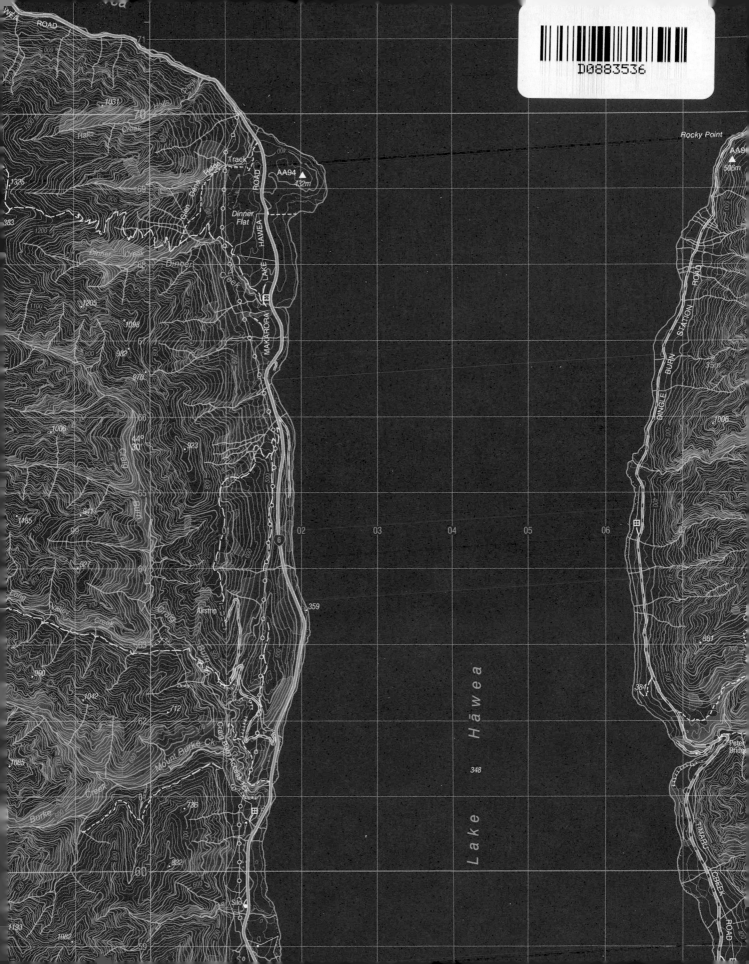

First published in 2017 by Beatnik Publishing

Copyright © 2017 Beatnik Publishing

Recipes: © 2017 Angelo Georgalli

Text: © 2017 Angelo Georgalli and Carla Munro

Photographs: © 2017 Sally Greer, with exception of photographs of Angelo on page 11, 14 & 22, © 2017 Levi Harrell, and photograph of Cardrona Valley Lodge, page 8 and photo of terrariums on page 170 © 2017 Jodie Rainsford

Shot on location at Cardrona Valley Lodge, Dingleburn Station and various locations in the Wanaka region.

Design, Typesetting & Cover: © 2017 Beatnik Publishing
Designers: Sally Greer, Kyle Ranudo & Kitki Tong

Endspaper Maps: © 2015 Land Information New Zealand
Topo50 Map CA13 – Lake Hawea (Edition 1.04 Published 2014) – front endpaper.
Topo50 Map CB12 – Cardrona (Edition 1.03 Published 2014) – back endpaper.

Printed and bound in China.

ISBN 978-0-9941383-5-4

Beatnik

PO Box 8276, Symonds Street,
Auckland 1150, New Zealand

www.beatnikpublishing.com

ANGELO'S
WILD KITCHEN
FAVOURITE FAMILY RECIPES

Beatnik

CONTENTS

INTRODUCTION

Food and family. It just doesn't get any better than that. When it comes down to it, no matter where you live or who you are, as long as you have food and family, you're doing all right.

My journey as The Game Chef has given me an epic opportunity to share my wild passion for the great outdoors and for great food with more than just my family – and for that I am forever grateful. So thanks guys, for coming on this adventure with me, and giving wild food a go.

I guess, for me, my Wild Food Philosophy (I'll tell you about that a bit later) has been a culmination of everything I've learned and experienced throughout my life. And to be honest, really became hugely important to me once Steph and I had our first baby.

When Luca was born I really started thinking, in the back of my mind, about the world and how it would impact his little life. You know, his world in the beginning was us – what we taught him, told him, fed him... we had that power to make sure he was getting the best we could.

But as our children grow up, I believe it is so important that we are teaching our kids to appreciate, to love and to be passionate about nature, the wild, the great outdoors – and real good food.

Growing up it was my mother and my father who created and nurtured this environment of love – love for me and my brothers, and love of cooking. Cooking together, fishing and foraging together, laughing and eating together. Now, as a Dad myself, there's nothing I love more than teaching my kids to cook, to fish, to hunt, to love and appreciate what they eat, where it comes from, and how it makes them healthy and happy.

And this is the thing I want to be really clear on in this book – it's not just about eating more green things and less stodge. Being healthy and happy comes from a much deeper place. It starts in the ground, in the plants, in the air, in the water we fish from.

It's about where the greens came from. Where your meat came from. What kind of state was the dirt in? What nutrients were in the soil? What were the animals eating? Were they happy, wild, and wandering free, grazing on real good grass? Were they stress-free? Or were their leaves, muscles, roots atrophied with stress, depleted and shriveled by nasty chemicals and additives?

Healthy living isn't just for us – it's for the food we eat.

You can fill your pantry with 'healthy' options and pat yourself on the back and say 'yep, I'm giving my kids the best fuel money can buy', but that's only a small part of it. To really get your kids to understand what it means to eat well, to live well, to make great choices and feel good inside and out, they need to know where their food is coming from and why fresh, local, and as wild as possible, is best.

And they need to get their hands dirty.

I remember the feeling of fresh, warm dough between my fingers. My mother's hands guiding me to knead, to pull, to press, and to stretch the dough. It was like a game. I loved it. I remember fishing with my Dad and him guiding my little hands into the mouth of the fish to remove the hook, scrubbing the scales off with a blunt blade. Did you bake with your mother when you were young? Did you beg to break the eggs into the bowl, your mother laughing and fishing out shards of shell with her fingers? Did you pull weeds and pick the peas with your Dad on Saturdays? Did you crack open the pod and lick the peas up one by one, crunching on sweet freshness? Ah, best of times, best of times.

This is what I'm talking about. Yeah, I love the hunting, fishing, gathering, foraging, cooking, and eating – but none of it would mean much without passing on the knowledge of what it all means to my kids. Bringing them with me, teaching them the 'how', guiding their understanding of the wilderness and how it can take care of them, feed them, nurture them. Why wild, fresh,

stress-free food is best. Guiding their capable, clever little hands as they tend their own garden, catch their own fish, raise their own chooks. They give it all meaning. They make it more fun. And they teach me a thing or two as well!

So what do I mean by 'stress-free' foods? Well, it's pretty easy when you think about it. Food, any food – veges, fruits, meat, grains, dairy – that is grown or raised, whether naturally in the wild or organically on a farm, ideally should come from an environment as natural as possible. Everything grows naturally where and when it's supposed to, seasonally, geographically. Imagine trying to force oranges to grow in the Arctic. If there was money in it you can bet some multinational company would probably figure out a way – and that's exactly what I'm trying to get across. There's no need for force-fed, force-grown, heat-treated, hormone-hyped produce. It simply doesn't taste as good.

I want to taste the earth in my veges. I want my meat tender, rich, pure, and bursting with healthy flavour. I want to taste wild blackberries in my bacon. I want my food to be happy. Make sense?

While travelling through Asia my wife, Steph, and I did a five-day cooking course in Chiang Mai. Now these guys know all about stress-free food. Everything we cooked came from the environment around us. We gathered, picked, foraged, plucked, and chased our ingredients and, under the guidance of these natural master chefs, created flavours that made our taste buds sing. The aroma of fresh herbs practically growing wild, stayed with us for days, in the air, ingrained into our skin – and it was pure magic! Sitting cross-legged in the dirt, cooking, sharing ideas, smelling, touching, tasting – laughing together, communicating not through language, but through the language of food, forming friendships and lifelong relationships with herbs and spices – it's an experience I'll never forget and that has influenced many of the flavours and recipes in this book.

Speaking of this book, it's a bit different to the first one – which I hope you have 'cos it's a bloody good one. This book is more about creating your own Wild Kitchen and bringing your family into it. I want to show you that a Wild Kitchen exists in every local grocer, butcher, backyard, and on every windowsill. It's about

what's important in living a healthy, fulfilling life. And believe me, I know about living an unhealthy life!

I was working too hard, too long, missing out on my kids' early lives, putting making money first then – bam – it hit me. Enough was enough. I had to get out. I had achieved so much, but what did that mean? The cafés, the restaurants, the accolades – what did they mean when my wife and kids hardly saw me, and when they did I was run down, zoned out, bled dry. I needed to figure out how to live again, how to cook and love it and still be there for my family – while providing for them as well! Haha, easy, right?

So I followed an intuitive path that led me here – to this book, to Cardrona, a stunning valley between Wanaka and Queenstown. To a healthy, amazing life with my family, living in paradise, hunting, fishing, gathering, growing, and guiding others in this gorgeous place to do the same. To *The Game Chef* and then further, into *Angelo's Wild Kitchen* and our luxury lodge in the Cardrona Valley.

Now, I'm not just cooking for people, I'm teaching and sharing and guiding from a beautiful lodge, where anyone is welcome to come and stay with us, to see how we live, to immerse themselves in our way of life, to learn and to share – or just to escape from the city like I needed to! From the hunting and fishing to the growing and cooking, our new Cardrona Valley Lodge offers visitors of all ages and nationalities the opportunity to spend time with me, living, learning and fully experiencing the Wild Kitchen life.

THE WILD KITCHEN PHILOSOPHY

When I was 12 years old, I shot my first hare. I'll never forget the joy on my father's face. The look he gave me, the firm, happy pat on my head, made my little heart swell with such pride, such happiness – man, I still get goose bumps! You see my Dad hadn't cooked fresh hare in over 30 years, since he was a young man on Cyprus. For him, this simple animal represented his history, his home, his roots and brought back memories filled with carefree freedom and good times. The taste of a dish from childhood does that, it takes you back immediately, and I'd done that for my father with a skinny English hare.

I guess if my Wild Kitchen philosophy started anywhere it was then, in the gleam of memories in my Dad's eyes as he skinned, prepped and cooked the best darn hare I ever tasted. Food isn't just about fueling our body. It's emotional. It's a language. It's a memory. It inspires feelings of joy, of gratitude, of sacredness. So it should be pure.

I talked quite a bit in my last book, *The Game Chef*, about my journey into food through my mother and fathers' passions for cooking from scratch. With their combined heritage being Cypriot Greek and Italian, I was kind of destined to follow my nose into the kitchen. An avid angler and cook, my Dad showed me how to fish, to prepare wild foods, to garden and to forage for veges even on the English commons and village streambeds. My mother gave me my love of flavour and creating from scratch. The way she tossed a fistful of flour on the wooden table, sprinkled a pinch, or two, or three, of pepper and salt into the mix, ripped a clutch of fresh basil and oregano, and tore it lovingly over her work in progress – it was an inspiration. She made cooking look like art, like a symphony being written before my eyes.

Plus, I knew from the age 14 that school wasn't going to do it for me. I kept gazing out the window planning my next hunting, fishing, camping trip. I left and worked in my cousin's deli to save for my own camping gear and fishing rig. And I started exploring.

This exploring lasted all my life and led me here, to today. Through travelling the world and learning about other cultures' foods, to competing in archery competitions – and winning – to moving to New Zealand and starting and selling several successful cafés and delis, it was all leading me here – to Cardrona, to the lodge, and to *Angelo's Wild Kitchen*. I feel like I'm finally home, like this is the calling I was searching for all that time.

I have to be totally honest. When I wrote *The Game Chef*, I wasn't completely living my own philosophy. I was still eating sugar, gluten, dairy – everything and anything that gave me the sense of being sated. Now, I'm not going to get all preachy, but there are foods out there that are basically liars. I could make some comparisons, but I think my publishers would slap me with a defamation clause...

As I was saying, I wasn't feeling awesome. Don't get me wrong, I loved my life – I'm bloody lucky and I know it – but I felt like crap inside. I was overweight, and I knew I wasn't being true to my beliefs. I was 'indulging' and guys, seriously, there's nothing wrong with that every now and then – it's kind of good for you actually. But too much of a good thing is never a good thing. So I reassessed where I was at with my health, my soul, and my goals in life.

All I had to do was to live what I believed, wholly and honestly.

And I believe in wild, foraged, local, fresh, seasonal foods that nourish all aspects of who we are as human beings – our physical body and cells, our brain and minds, and our spirit or soul or whatever you call it, maybe your consciousness or conscience. Food that is stress free, grown naturally, raised lovingly, or is wild and free, tastes better, is better for us and for nature on every level, and provides us with the optimum health overall.

The Wild Kitchen philosophy incorporates my love of the great outdoors, the wilderness and the places that take us back to a primal level of existence, with my love of beautiful, natural, healthy food. My beautiful, indulgent wife, Steph, has allowed me to really explore what this means and how to share it with others – including our kids. And now, through this book, and through our new lodge, Cardrona Valley Lodge, I'm sharing the Wild Kitchen philosophy with you.

TIPS AND TRICKS –
HOW TO BRING THE WILD INTO ANY HOME

I know not everyone can live in the country. Some people wouldn't even want to, and that's cool. Each to their own, and each to their own way of life.

But here's the thing – even an apartment dweller can bring elements of my Wild Kitchen philosophy into their snazzy inner-city pad. Here's some of my tips and tricks to bringing the wild into any home...

POT PLANTS!

Guys, pot plants are great! They can be any size, fit anywhere, and don't need a huge amount of time and energy to keep healthy. So – make your pot plants edible! Grow herbs, chillies, baby tomatoes, spinach, just about anything you can think of, can be grown in a pot. Keeping your potted garden stress free is easy! Don't smoke around them. Talk or sing to them. Check with a garden expert on the best way to care for them. They'll be happy, and give you happy food!

YOUR LOCAL ORGANIC WHOLEFOOD STORE

Most cities, and even smaller towns, have a local wholefood store. It's their passion to find the best-quality wholefoods so we don't have to. Wholefood stores are full of organic produce and products – just make sure to check the labels to find out where it came from. I like to keep as close to home as possible – less carbon footprints left behind!

FARMERS' MARKETS!

Man, I love a good farmers' market! And the great news – they've become trendy! About time! Back in the day everyone travelled to the local village market to barter and trade goods, services and produce...yeah, well now they're back – only, you're unlikely to be able to trade your pig for five fat hens and a sack of barley. Farmers' markets are the best because usually people are selling their own homemade, homegrown goods – and that's awesome for everyone! Three cheers for the farmers' markets!

YOUR LOCAL BUTCHER

Have a hunt around your neighbourhood for your closest local butcher, and get to know them. Ask them about their wares, the farms their meat came from, if any of it is wild. Chat to them about the cuts, their methods, ask their advice – these guys love to be appreciated, and they should be! A good butcher is almost as good as raising your own animals.

GET SUPERMARKET SAVVY

Supermarkets these days are joining the real food revolution and most of them have really great organic and wholefood sections. They also have good delis and butchers and are buying local where at all possible. When you're in your local supermarket, choose produce that is labelled 'organic' or has been grown as locally as possible. For example – if you have a choice between a locally grown orange and an orange grown on the other side of the world – choose the local one! And remember, packaged foods generally have additives – read the labels!

THE WEEK AHEAD

Trust me, I know eating healthy can sometimes seem like a pain in the proverbial, but it can be done, it is worth it, and it can be made a whole lot easier if you're prepared. It just takes a bit of thought – and it can be fun!

Sit down on a Sunday night – maybe over dinner – and talk through the week ahead with the family. What does everyone feel like eating? What's in the garden? What's in season at the grocer? Make a family menu, get the kids involved, give them pens and paper, make it fun.

This is also a great way to plan one-on-one time with the family. Maybe one of the kids gets to come to the shops with you, another gets to hang out and help you harvest veges and herbs from the garden, another gets to roll the homemade pasta... However you can spend time with your kids one-on-one, it goes a long, long way to creating a strong and healthy relationship with each of them.

Use this cookbook to prep readymade, fresh sauces, butters, and rubs that can be utilised in many of my dishes – and you can even create some of your own! Then you've got fresh, homemade goodness in your fridge to whip up something scrumptious in a heartbeat.

Here's why prepping for the week ahead is awesome:

- You have time to plan healthy meals that are fast, easy and delicious!

- You know what to get at the supermarket, the grocer, the butcher, the garden, the freezer – no more panic cooking!

- You'll enjoy the meal more because it'll be cooked from scratch fresh.

- Your evenings are a joy rather than a mad, tired rush.

Make it easy for yourself and your family. Create time to be together in the kitchen, the garden, the outdoors, and make cooking the family meals a fun, happy time you will all look back on with love and joy.

WHAT'S IN YOUR PANTRY?
YOUR WILD KITCHEN SHOPPING LIST

Don't you hate it when you've set your heart on a recipe and you start cooking and – darn! You don't have any turmeric! Yeah, me too. Ha, it happens to the best of us! So I've created a list of essential ingredients for the Wild Kitchen…

OILS

- avocado oil
- canola oil
- coconut oil
- corn oil
- extra virgin olive oil
- flaxseed oil
- grapeseed oil
- peanut oil
- rice bran oil
- sesame seed oil
- sunflower oil

VINEGARS

- balsamic vinegar
- malt vinegar
- manuka honey cider vinegar
- raw apple cider vinegar
- red wine vinegar
- rice vinegar

DRIED HERBS

- basil
- bay leaf
- chives
- coriander
- dill weed
- kaffir lime leaves
- marjoram
- oregano
- parsley
- rosemary
- sage
- tarragon
- thyme

DRIED FRUITS

- apples
- apricots
- banana chips
- blueberries
- cranberries
- dates
- figs
- mangoes
- nectarines
- peaches
- pears
- pineapple
- plums
- prunes
- raspberries
- red currants
- raisins

NUTS

- almond nuts
- brazil nuts
- cashew nuts
- chestnuts
- cocoa nuts
- hazelnuts
- macadamia nuts
- pine nuts
- pistachio nuts
- peanuts
- walnuts

SEEDS

- flaxseeds
- pomegranate seeds
- poppy seeds
- pumpkin seeds
- sesame seeds
- sunflower seeds

SPICES

- black pepper
- black sesame seeds
- cardamom
- caraway seeds
- chilli flakes
- chilli powder
- chinese five spice
- cinnamon
- cloves
- coriander seeds
- cumin
- dill seeds
- fennel seeds
- ginger (fresh and powdered)
- juniper berries
- lemon pepper

- moroccan spice
- nutmeg
- pink peppercorns
- sesame seeds
- star anise
- sumac
- hot smoked paprika
- sweet smoked paprika
- paprika
- saffron
- turmeric
- vanilla pod

FLOURS

- almond flour
- all-purpose flour
- arrowroot
- buckwheat flour
- coconut flour
- cornflour
- chickpea flour
- gluten-free flour
- potato flour
- rice flour
- semolina flour
- self-raising flour
- soya flour
- wholewheat flour

GRAINS & RICES

- brown rice
- black rice
- bulgur
- bran millet
- couscous
- cornmeal
- polenta
- rice
- wild rice

LEGUMES

- black-eyed beans
- broad beans
- black beans
- borlotti beans
- butter beans
- cannellini beans
- chickpeas
- fava beans
- kidney beans
- lentils
- lupin beans
- peas
- soya beans
- split peas
- white beans

SAUCES

- black bean sauce
- chilli pepper sauce
- fish sauce
- maple syrup
- molasses/ pomegranate syrup
- oyster sauce
- plum sauce
- Tabasco
- teriyaki sauce
- soy sauce
- sweet chilli sauce
- worcestershire sauce

OTHERS

- capers
- canned tomatoes
- dijon mustard
- english mustard
- gherkins
- gluten-free bread crumbs
- panko breadcrumbs
- savoiardi biscuits for tiramisu
- sun-dried tomatoes
- vanilla extract
- whole grain mustard
- yeast

BREAKFAST

How you start the day sets up how you're going to go through it. If you start the day with a healthy, fresh, delicious, nutritious breakfast, your body, mind and whatever you call your soul, will want more of the same. Plus, a healthy start to the day doesn't mean cringing through a bowl of plain porridge (although I happen to think plain porridge is awesome). My recipes for a real good breakfast have got the Wild Kitchen seal of approval as well as being absolutely YUM!

Here's a tip – for a healthy start everyday make a bunch of extras on the weekend – such as the hash browns – and pop them in the freezer.

EGGS BENNY WITH SALMON

How many times have I been in a café and heard people order the Eggs Benny? Hundreds? It's a fave, that's for darn sure, so here's my take on it, Angelo's Eggs Benny…

Hash Browns (see page 29)

Hollandaise Sauce (see page 48)

Poached Eggs (See page 28)

1L **water**

4 drops of **lemon juice**

Pinch of **salt**

Pinch of **pepper**

1 sprig of **dill** – plus extra to garnish

90g **salmon**

Half a handful of fresh **baby spinach leaves**

Prepare the hash browns or grab what you need from your freezer! While these wee tattie gems are in the oven, prepare the eggs and hollandaise, and set aside. The trick to a great hollandaise – don't stress about it and follow my recipe on page 48.

In a saucepan, boil the water, drop in the lemon juice, a pinch of salt and a pinch of pepper, and add the dill. Once the water is at boiling point and turn down to a simmer, place the salmon in to poach. Poach for 3 minutes.

Blanch the baby spinach in hot water for 20 seconds, then dab dry with a paper towel.

ARRANGEMENT

For a gorgeous, traditional look to impress your brekkie guests, stack your hash browns in the middle of the plate, one on top of the other. Lay the salmon on top of that, then your eggs. Serve the wilted spinach on the side. Brilliant!

Liberally pour your perfect hollandaise over the stack of goodness. Add salt and pepper to taste, garnish with extra dill and voila! Better than a café!

POACHED EGGS

Okay, okay, you might be thinking to yourself, "why the heck is Angelo trying to tell me how to poach eggs? I know how to poach an egg!" And you probably do – everyone likes their eggs a certain way. A friend of mine orders her poached eggs as "slightly firm in the middle with no runny whites, please…" Fussy! Haha, but really we all have a way we like our eggs – this is mine…

1L **water**

1 Tbsp **white vinegar**

2 fresh **eggs** (preferably from your own chooks!)

Bring water to boiling point in a deep saucepan.

Make a 'whirlpool' in the pan. Add the white vinegar.

Add eggs. Turn heat down to simmer and cook to your liking.

Boom!

TIP – The best way to poach an egg is to crack them into a bowl, create a whirlpool as fast as you can and then drop the two eggs into the whirlpool.

HASH BROWNS

I have used this recipe for many years, and they were an absolute fave GF brekkie at all my cafés. Use them to replace bread for yummy GF options, like with my Eggs Benny (see page 26). Agria potatoes are the best – the texture is spot on! Make a bunch of them and keep in the fridge or freezer – great for hungry kids after school!

1kg **Agria potatoes** – unpeeled and halved

6 Tbsp **olive oil**

1 large **white onion** – finely chopped

½ **red onion** – finely chopped

1 tsp **salt**

1 tsp **pepper**

Place potatoes in a saucepan of boiling water and cook for 15 minutes until half cooked. Blanch in cold water, then grate using a standard grater. Set aside.

Heat 3 tablespoons oil over a high heat in a large pan. Add onions and sprinkle with salt and pepper. Cook onions through until lightly browned, then set aside to cool in a bowl.

While the onions are cooling, preheat the oven to 190°C on fanbake.

Combine onions with grated potatoes. Use a wooden spoon to gently toss through. Be gentle/careful not to turn into mash potatoes! You want these hash browns to be fluffy not dense.

Get a bowl of lukewarm water for dipping your hands in – you'll see what I mean…

Coat hands in water and then pick up a handful of potato mix (approx 80g) and shape into a round hash brown and pop aside.

Coat the bottom of a large pan with the remaining 3 tablespoons olive oil and heat over high heat. Pop hash browns into pan and brown off both sides. It will take at least two batches to get through all the hash browns – depending on pan size.

Place fried hash browns on a baking tray and pop in oven for 8 minutes. And they're ready to use, refrigerate or freeze! Happy hashing!

BANANA RICE BREAKFAST PUDDING

For this hearty breakfast pudding I've used Arborio rice, but you could use any leftover rice you might have from the night before. It's such a warming, wholesome, and tasty start to the day. Make sure you're stirring the rice constantly to stop it sticking to the pan – no one likes scrubbing burned rice off their cookware!

1 cup **Arborio** or **short grain rice**

2 cups **coconut milk**

1 cup **boiling water**

¼ tsp **vanilla bean extract** or **vanilla essence**

¼ tsp **cinnamon**

1 Tbsp **chia seeds**

1 tsp **poppy seeds**

½ Tbsp **coconut oil**

2 uppeeled **bananas** – sliced on an angle

1 Tbsp **coconut sugar**

GARNISH

Black sesame seeds

Into a medium saucepan add rice, 1½ cups of coconut milk, and water and bring to a boil. Once boiling, turn heat down to a simmer. Make sure you stir constantly.

Add vanilla bean extract and stir.

Add cinnamon, chia seeds, poppy seeds and stir.

Simmer at a low heat for 25–30 minutes, stirring.

Into a large pan add coconut oil, then add sliced banana, sprinkle with coconut sugar and fry on both sides until golden brown.

Add remaining coconut milk – stir carefully, trying not to mash or squash the banana, until thickened to a nice saucy consistency.

Remove bananas and keep the sauce that is left in the pan for pouring over the rice. Garnish with black sesame seed and serve. Yum!

GF SPICED COCONUT FRUIT LOAF

So free of anything naughty, so full of everything yummy – this is a breakfast loaf you can really sink your teeth into. I love the multitude of flavours in this loaf and the kids do too. It's sweet enough naturally that they think its an absolute treat!

½ cup **raisins**

½ cup **cranberries**

½ cup **dates** – chopped

½ cup **coconut thread**

½ cup **chocolate** or **cacao nibs**

½ cup **crystallised ginger** – chopped

½ cup **dried apricots** – chopped

1 **orange** – zest, peeled then blended

½ tsp **turmeric**

½ tsp **cinnamon**

½ tsp **cardamon**

½ tsp **allspice**

325ml **warm water**

150ml **warm coconut milk**

2 tsp **yeast**

½ cup **coconut sugar**

½ **vanilla pod** – scraped seeds

½ tsp **salt**

1 cup **whole walnuts**

½ cup **pumpkin seeds**

2½ cups **GF self-raising flour**, plus extra ½ cup for dusting and kneading

1 cup **coconut flour**

Icing sugar – to dust

In a large bowl add raisins, cranberries, dates, coconut thread, chocolate or cacao nibs, crystallised ginger and dried apricots. Add the orange zest, then peel the zested orange, blend the flesh and add the blended flesh to the bowl. Add spices (turmeric, cinnamon, cardamon and allspice) Leave the mixture to soak in juice for 30 minutes.

Place water and coconut milk in another bowl and mix in yeast then add sugar, vanilla and salt. Leave aside for 15 minutes. Add to the fruit mixture.

Add walnuts and pumpkin seeds. Mix through. Add flours and mix through.

Dust a bench with the extra flour. Place mixture on bench, knead and form into a loaf shape.

Place baking paper on an oven tray. Place loaf on paper. Loosely cover with cling film, a plastic bag or a damp tea towel. Leave in a warm room or area for 2 hours.

When ready to bake, preheat the oven to 180°C and bake loaf for 45 minutes. Remove and place on an airing rack to cool.

Dust with icing sugar when cool.

You might want to eat it as it is or add a topping like fresh berries or yoghurt or hazelnut butter – however you eat it, enjoy!

15 min 20 min Serves 1    GF   NF

ANGELO'S SUPER-DUPER BREAKFAST

Eggs are a superfood. Turmeric is superfood. Combining these two incredible superfoods makes for a pretty super-duper breakfast. A super way to start the day.

ROAST TOMATOES

2 ripened **vine tomatoes**

2 Tbsp **extra virgin olive oil**

½ Tbsp **balsamic vinegar**

Himalayan salt and **black pepper**

TURMERIC EGGS

2 Tbsp **extra virgin olive oil**

2 pinches **turmeric**

Pinch of **black pepper**

½ Tbsp **balsamic vinegar**

2 **eggs**

TO SERVE

Creamy Mushrooms Sauce (see page 52)

Turkish bread or your own personal fave

Hash Browns (see page 29)

Preheat the oven to 180°C.

Place tomatoes in a skillet/ovenproof dish and sprinkle with extra virgin olive oil, balsamic vinegar and, a pinch each of salt. Place in oven to roast for 15 minutes.

While tomatoes are roasting, make the turmeric eggs.

Heat oil in a large ovenproof saucepan. Sprinkle over turmeric and black pepper. Add balsamic vinegar. Swirl to mix.

Crack the eggs carefully into the hot pan, and fry off until the base of eggs are crispy.

Place saucepan with eggs in oven for 1 minute.

Remove tomatoes and eggs from oven and serve with creamy mushrooms, bread or hash browns.

5-7 min   10–20 min   Serves 3–5   DF   GF   NF

COCONUT & CRANBERRY PANCAKES

Using the oven makes the pancakes rise a wee bit more without burning the outside.

1 cup **coconut flour**

1 cup **GF flour**

½ cup **coconut sugar**

¼ cup **coconut thread**

½ cup **cranberries**

2½ **banana** – peeled

1 **egg**

3 Tbsp **coconut yoghurt**

1 cup **warm water**

½ tsp **vanilla essence**

2 cups **coconut milk**

1 Tbsp **coconut oil** (for each batch cooked in the pan)

TO SERVE

Maple syrup

Coconut yoghurt

Coconut chips

Cinnamon

Preheat the oven to 180°C.

Mix all dry ingredients together in a large bowl then add 1½ bananas, egg, coconut yoghurt, water and vanilla essence, mixing as you add the wet ingredients. Slice the remaining banana and set aside.

Heat 2 tablespoons of coconut oil in a pan then drop in 3 tablespoons of mixture to make 1 pancake into the pan. You should be able to fit 3 pancakes into the pan at the same time – or just go at your own pace.

Add 2 reserved banana slices to the top wet side of each pancake. Once golden brown on the underside, turn and cook the banana side for 1 minute then pop in the oven for 3–4 minutes.

Present on a plate and add your favourite toppings to serve.

TIP – If pan dries out add more coconut oil before cooking the next batch. The pancakes will soak up the oil.

BUTTERS & BASES

I love to create the bases for the dishes I know I'll make during the week ahead of time – you'll know that if you read The Week Ahead section! These recipes feature as staples in other recipes throughout the book, but can also be used as you wish. Go on, get creative! Cook by feel, by taste, explore, have fun. Imagine what it might taste like, play with it – cooking is all about adventure, learning, trial and error. Don't be afraid to get inventive!

CHILLI BUTTER

Oh I do love butter and we now know that butter's better for you than sugar, and my Chilli Butter is even better! This stuff is great on anything – breads, crackers, potatoes, dolloped onto pizza, just about anything! Cook with it in your pan to add a real zing of flavour to your meats!

150g **butter** – room temperature or softened

1 whole **chilli** – sliced seeds and all

1 Tbsp **fresh coriander leaves** – chopped

½ tsp **sumac**

¼ tsp **turmeric**

Mix all ingredients together. Place in container and use as above. Keeps for up to 2 weeks in the fridge.

SPICY HERB BUTTER

Spicy and herby might sound a bit much – but trust me, this butter is melt-in-your-mouth good! Use it for just about anything – it'll turn any old piece of bread into a slice fit for a king. It's also really pretty and looks good in little rolls on a slab of schist or wood on the table to impress dinner guests!

1 tsp **coriander seeds**

1 tsp **cumin seeds**

1 tsp **turmeric**

1 tsp **smoked paprika**

1 tsp **sumac**

150g **butter**

2 cloves **garlic**

7 large **basil leaves**

1 tsp **oregano leaves**

1 tsp **thyme**

½ tsp **black pepper**

½ tsp **Himalayan salt**

Put all ingredients into a bowl and mix thoroughly together. Keep in fridge and use as you wish!

CLASSIC ITALIAN PESTO

I've been using this recipe for 25 years, in all my cafés and restaurants, and have never changed it. Usually I would make 2 litres at a time but this recipe is scaled down for the home. A great pesto is one of the most versatile bases you can have in the fridge to add to dishes, eat on crackers, put in a sandwich or wrap. Pesto is such a refreshing flavour and is full of goodness.

1 clove **garlic**

50g toasted **pine nuts**

2 handfuls of **basil leaves**

¾ cup **extra virgin olive oil**

¼ cup **powdered Parmesan**

½ Tbsp **lemon juice**

Salt and **pepper**

Blend garlic and pine nuts in a food processor. Use a spatula between blending to push the pine nuts down from the edges and corners.

Remove basil leaves from stalks and add to food processor. Blend.

Add olive oil, add Parmesan, lemon juice and a pinch of salt and pepper. Blend everything until it's a fine consistency. Put into a clean glass jar and store in fridge for multi-purpose use!

TIP – Parsley can be used with the basil – try a handful of each.

ALL THINGS SAUCY

Just like Butters & Bases chapter, All Things Saucy provides you with some staple sauces that can be kept in your fridge to use during your weekly meals. These feature throughout the *Wild Kitchen* cookbook, but, like the butters and bases, can be used on just about anything! As I said before, get creative, feel your way to the right flavours, and enjoy experimenting! Sauces really do change the flavour, the integrity, of a meal. They can turn a simple meal into an Asian fusion sensation, or a Greek revival, or an Italian masterpiece. So go get saucy!

HOLLANDAISE SAUCE

Oh the mighty hollandaise that has brought grown men to tears! Yes, it can be a trickster, but stay calm, follow these steps, and keep your whisking light and quick, and you'll be right. Hollandaise is a buttery sauce I could say was invented in France, but I might be wrong as there is some debate about it being a Dutch sauce for fish. Hollandaise on fish, aye, what a great idea!

75g **butter**

1 tsp **white vinegar**

2 **egg yolks**

Pinch of **black pepper**

4 drops of **lemon juice**

Melt the butter in a stainless steel or copper bowl resting over a saucepan of hot water on the stove.

In another bowl add vinegar, black pepper and egg yolks. Switch out the bowls, placing the egg bowl over the hot water.

Whisk through the mix gently as you slowly drizzle in the butter. As soon as sauce is smooth – STOP! Don't over whisk or over heat. The secret to a great Hollandaise is timing.

Add lemon juice and stir through gently – a couple of swirls is enough!

CHERRY SAUCE/BASE

This is a good base to make sauces, glazes and to add to jus. It's perfect for desserts, meats and poultry and has a beautiful, gentle spice to it.

600g **cherries**

250ml **water**

6 whole **cloves**

1 tsp **powdered** or **ground ginger**

1 tsp **allspice**

Place cherries and water in a medium pot over a medium heat. Add cloves, ginger and allspice.

Simmer for 35 minutes. Remove from heat – allow to cool and pick out any stones.

When cool, place in a blender (make sure there are no stones) and blend into a sauce consistency. Jar it up and refrigerate.

NAPOLETANA SAUCE

This is my Mum's recipe. What I really love about this recipe is that it tastes better every day – up to 7 days! It's one of the most versatile Italian sauces of them all and once it's made you can use it for pasta or over chicken. The sauce itself takes a bit of time to cook, but you can use it in just about anything and you can freeze it for later use as well! Imagine – little frozen tubs of homemade Napoletana Sauce in the freezer for that perfect Italian dinner! And the good news – you know exactly what went into it!

¼ cup **extra virgin olive oil**

3 cloves **garlic** – whole and peeled

5 x 400g cans of crushed **tomatoes** or if you have an abundance of fresh toms, great! Use those! Around 4-5kgs is perfect!

1 Tbsp **tomato purée**

1 Tbsp **oregano leaves** – dry or fresh

3 large **basil leaves** – chopped

1 cup **stock** – vegetable or chicken

Salt and **pepper**

Heat a large pot over a high heat. Add olive oil and garlic and fry until golden brown.

Add tomatoes, tomato purée, oregano and basil. Then add stock and season with salt and pepper.

Leave to simmer over a low heat for 2.5–3 hours.

Use straightaway in a pasta dish or leave to cool and put in the fridge or freezer to use later. Easy! Homemade napoletana sauce !

CREAMY MUSHROOM SAUCE

This delicious, creamy mushroomy sauce is a fantastic base for plenty of dishes or to have as a topping. Serve as is on steaks, chicken, or pasta and you have an instant, wholesome meal. I've used white button mushrooms in this recipe, but you can use whatever kind of mushrooms you prefer – each has a lightly unique flavour.

30g **butter**

2 cloves **garlic**

260g **mushrooms** – thickly sliced

3 Tbsp **extra virgin olive oil**

60ml **white wine**

100ml **chicken stock**

150ml **cream**

2 good pinches of **thyme** – fresh or dried

1 tsp **arrowroot** or **cornflour**

1 Tbsp **water**

2 Tbsp grated **Parmesan**

Salt and **pepper**

Place butter and garlic in a saucepan and sauté over a high heat. Once garlic has browned off, add mushrooms. When the mushroom have absorbed the butter add the olive oil and stir through mushrooms.

Brown mushrooms on both sides and then add wine. Cook until the wine has evaporated then add the chicken stock and cream.

Add thyme. Bring to a boil then reduce heat and simmer over a medium heat. Mix arrowroot or cornflour with water and add to mushrooms to thicken. Turn heat off.

Add Parmesan and salt and pepper to taste. Stir through and serve.

TIP – If you are DF you can use olive oil instead of butter and coconut milk instead of cream and simply skip the Parmesan. If you're vegetarian use vegetable stock.

BBQ SAUCE

My kids love to coat everything in this amazing, yummy BBQ sauce, and because it's homemade, you know it's good for them. There is a bit of sugar in BBQ Sauce, but hey, a little bit of something sweet is totally fine in moderation! Just don't drink it.

1½ cups **soft brown sugar** or **coconut sugar**

1½ cups **Napoletan**a **Sauce** (see page 50)

½ cup **red wine vinegar**

½ cup **water**

½ cup diced **prunes**

1½ Tbsp **Worcestershire sauce**

3 Tbsp **wholegrain mustard**

1 Tbsp **hot chilli pepper sauce**

1 tsp **smoked paprika**

½ tsp **salt**

½ tsp **pepper**

In a saucepan, mix brown sugar, napoletana sauce , red wine vinegar, water and prunes. Bring to a boil and simmer, stirring regularly.

Add Worcestershire sauce, wholegrain mustard, hot chilli pepper sauce, smoked paprika, and salt and pepper and stir through briskly.

Serve with meat dishes or on pizza. This sauce can be bottled and stored in the fridge for up to a week.

PLUM SAUCE

Another fantastic sauce you can prepare on a Sunday and keep in the fridge for a week. Use it on meats, pastas fish, pizza – just about anything! Plum sauce is great in Asian fusion cooking and also goes brilliantly on pizza with smoked chicken and brie! This sauce also has amazing good stuff in it such as turmeric and apple cider vinegar – both are really good for your digestive and lymphatic systems.

10 cups **plums**

1 medium **beetroot** – chopped into small pieces

1½ **onions** – finely chopped

1 tsp **chilli flakes**

1¾ cups **water**

4 cloves **roasted garlic** – minced

1 tsp finely chopped **ginger**

¾ cup **brown** or **coconut sugar**

½ cup **white rice vinegar**

½ cup **apple cider vinegar**

½ tsp **salt**

½ tsp **ground coriander**

½ tsp **turmeric**

Halve the plums and remove the stones.

In a large pot, combine the plums, beetroot, onions, chilli flakes, water, garlic, and ginger and simmer for 30 minutes until the plums and onions have completely softened.

Strain through a colander into a clean pot, squishing the mixture through with a spoon. Get as much juice out of the mixture as possible.

Place pot on stove, add all the other ingredients, and bring to a boil then simmer for a further 35 minutes until thickened.

Bottle and use!

BLACKBERRY SAUCE

I love blackberries! They remind me of being a kid and foraging for wild blackberries in England. I'd come home all stained with dark purple-red juice and my mother would be furious with me for the stains on my clothes. Ahhh, good times. Blackberries grow wild in New Zealand in many places, but you really do have to be careful in case they've been sprayed. Look for dead foliage around the bush. As with all wild foods, if in doubt – don't eat it!

20g **butter**

120g **blackberries** – freshly picked if possible!

¼ cup **sugar**

Zest of ¼ a **lemon**

1 Tbsp **red wine vinegar**

Salt and **pepper**

Pinch of **sumac**

Pinch of **cayenne pepper**

1 Tbsp **fresh sage** or 5 **sage leaves**

Heat the butter in a small pot over a medium heat.

Add blackberries, sugar, lemon zest, red wine vinegar, pinch of salt and pepper, sumac, cayenne pepper, and sage.

Simmer for 5 minutes until sauce thickens then take off heat and squash half the blackberries, leaving the other half whole because YUM!

MAYONNAISE

A simple, plain mayonnaise can be used on so many things – even dishes and foods you might not think about! I had a mate who would put mayonnaise on a slice of ham, roll it up, and pretend he was sucking on a cigar! See, just about anything! In England mayonnaise is often served with hot chips! This is one of the easiest mayonnaise recipes I know, and it's bloody good!

3 **eggs**

300ml **canola oil**, **vegetable oil** or **light olive oil**

Salt and **pepper**

Break eggs into a blender. Pop the lid on securely and blend.

Continue to blend and slowly drizzle in oil until the right consistency is achieved.

Add salt and pepper to taste and stir through.

Place in fridge for an hour. Refrigerate and use within 5 days.

TIP – use 1 egg for every 100ml of oil

MANGO MAYONNAISE

This versatile, tasty mayonaise is absolutely fantastic with poultry and prawns. Of course, you can use it on other things as well, and it really does go brilliantly with a fresh green salad.

2 **eggs**

1 clove **garlic**

1 tsp **wholegrain mustard**

200ml **canola oil**, **vegetable oil** or **light olive oil**

100g canned **mango**

¼ cup canned **mango juice** (from the same can!)

Salt and **pepper**

Break eggs into a blender. Add garlic and mustard.

Pop the lid on securely and blend. Continue to blend and slowly drizzle in oil until the right consistency is achieved. Add mango and canned mango juice, salt and pepper to taste and blend once more.

Place in fridge for an hour. Refrigerate and use within 5 days.

AIOLI

Aioli has become a staple in restaurants and cafés these days, but I've been loving me a good, homemade aioli since I was a whippersnapper. Of course, it's not an Italian or Greek recipe, aioli originated in Provence in France and Catalonia in Spain, and is often thought to be these regions' version of mayonnaise. It's not. It's a delicious, creamy, garlicky sauce that can be used – again – on just about anything.

2 **eggs**

1 clove **roasted garlic**

1 tsp **wholegrain mustard**

200ml **canola oil**, **vegetable oil** or **light olive oil**

Salt and **pepper**

¼ cup **powdered Parmesan**

1 tsp **lemon juice**

Break eggs into a blender. Add garlic and mustard.

Pop the lid on tight and blend. Continue to blend and slowly drizzle in oil until the right consistency is achieved.

Add salt and pepper to taste, the Parmesan and lemon juice and stir through.

Place in fridge for an hour. Refrigerate and use within 5 days.

CAESAR DRESSING

Julius Caesar invented this dressing for his own personal use – no, I'm kidding! This dressing is a take on the famous Caesar Salad invented by Caesar Cardini, an Italian in Mexico. One night when his restaurant kitchen supplies were running low, Caesar did what any great chef does and experimented, creating something delicious out of what he had left. The salad since became famous and hit LA in around 1925, and it's been popular ever since all over the world. Ave Caesar!

2 **eggs**

1 clove **roasted garlic**

1 tsp **wholegrain mustard**

4 **anchovies**

10 **capers**

¼ cup **powdered Parmesan**

1 tsp **lemon juice**

200ml **canola oil**, **vegetable oil** or **light olive oil**

Salt and **pepper**

Break eggs into a blender. Add garlic, mustard, anchovies, capers, powered Parmesan and lemon juice.

Pop the lid on tight and blend. Continue to blend and slowly drizzle in oil until the right consistency is achieved.

Add salt and pepper to taste and stir through.

Place in fridge for an hour. Refrigerate and use within 5 days.

SWEET CHILLI SAUCE

8 fresh **red chillies** – chopped

4 cloves **garlic**

20g finely grated **ginger**

½ cup **white vinegar** or **Asian-style vinegar**

1½ cups **brown sugar**

2½ cups **water**

¼ tsp **salt**

1 tsp **arrowroot**

2 Tbsp **water**

Put all ingredients except arrowroot and water into a blender, once blended add to pot and bring to a boil for 15 minutes.

Add the arrowroot mixed with water to thicken.

Leave to cool, then bottle. Will keep in fridge for 3 weeks.

GRAZING

Some foodie philosophies discuss the health benefits of grazing throughout the day, eating smaller meals up to five or six times a day. I don't know about that, I think each to their own, you know how you like to eat, and as long as it's as healthy, wholesome, fresh, and locally seasonal as possible, eat whenever you like! But here's some of my favourite grazing dishes that are just perfect to nibble when the mood strikes!

30 min   10–15 min   Serves 2   DF   GF   NF

VENISON BURGER

Now here's the important thing you need to understand about my wild recipes – you can use other meat! You could replace the venison with beef, lamb, chicken, even tofu or a big juicy slice of eggplant if you fancy. You can make this burger any way you like and it will still be a Wild Kitchen fave!

VENISON BURGER

1 Tbsp **extra virgin olive oil**

Pinch of **turmeric**

Pinch of **cinnamon**

Pinch of **smoked paprika**

1 tsp **thyme**

1 tsp **rosemary**

Salt and **pepper**

½ **white onion** – chopped

1 clove **garlic** – chopped

1 Tbsp **coconut sugar**

250g **minced venison**

1 **egg**

1 Tbsp **tomato paste**

¼ cup GF **breadcrumbs**

3 **prunes** – chopped

TO SERVE

Burger Bun (GF bun or bread of your choice, or my Hash Browns, see page 29)

Aioli – a hearty dollop (see page 62)

Handful of **watercress**

2 slices of **vine-ripened tomato**

6 slices of **mixed chargrilled capsicum**

1 Tbsp **BBQ Sauce** (see page 54)

3 slices of fried **mushrooms**

Preheat a medium size pan. Add oil, turmeric, cinnamon, smoked paprika, thyme, rosemary, salt, pepper, onion and garlic and sauté until onion is soft. Then add coconut sugar and caramelise the mixture until nice and golden. Set aside and leave to cool for a few minutes.

Put the minced venison, egg, tomato paste, GF breadcrumbs and prunes in a bowl and mix well – I use my hands! Then add the slightly cooled caramelised mixture and mix in.

Shape the mixture into 2 patties, then cook on the barbecue grill or in a hot pan with some oil until cooked to your liking.

The Wild Kitchen burger is a guaranteed hunger-buster. To assemble it, start with your bottom half of your bun (you can literally use any kind of bread for this – or even use one of my hash browns for a tasty gluten-free alternative!)

Smear your dollop of aioli on the upside of your bottom bun half then pile on the rest of the ingredients in order, finishing with an aioli smeared top half of bun – and you're done! Enjoy!

DEEP-FRIED VENISON SCOTCH EGGS

"Born in Scotland so ya know – scotch eggs"

These awesome little beauties are perfect on a long hike or hunt. They're protein-packed and absolutely delicious. Great for lunches or grazing, these bad boys will keep you going all day.

10 **eggs**

1 Tbsp **olive oil**

½ **onion** – sliced

1 clove **garlic** – diced

¼ **red capsicum/pepper** – chopped

1 tsp real **maple syrup**

500g **minced venison** (you can use minced beef or lamb or chicken as well!)

1 tsp **fresh thyme** – chopped

1 tsp **fresh rosemary** – chopped

1 tsp **fresh sage** – chopped

1 Tbsp **fresh parsley** – chopped

½ tsp **cinnamon**

½ tsp **turmeric**

½ tsp **coarse black pepper** or **pepper seasoning**

½ tsp **paprika**

1 tsp of **salt**

2 cups **GF breadcrumbs**

1 Tbsp **GF soy sauce**

4 Tbsp **GF flour**

Place 8 eggs in a saucepan of water, bring to boil and boil for 4–5 minutes – 10 minutes if you want hard-boiled eggs. Run under cold water for 15 minutes. Set aside.

Heat olive oil in a medium pan over a high heat and fry onion, garlic and red capsicum/pepper. Once onions have browned off, add maple syrup to caramelise the onions. Take off heat and set aside.

In a bowl, combine minced venison, fresh and dry herbs and spices and salt. Add 1 cup of GF breadcrumbs, 1 egg, and soy sauce. Pour in onion mixture and mix together.

Heat oil in a deep fryer to 180°C.

Peel boiled eggs and roll each in GF flour. Use floured hands to make 8 patties from the venison mixture and use to wrap each egg and seal. Lightly beat the remaining egg in a bowl and roll each wrapped egg in the beaten egg then in the remaining GF breadcrumbs. Repeat one more time.

Place in fryer for 5 minutes. Serve hot or cold.

TIP – if you don't have a deep fryer you can add a cup or two of coconut oil to a deep wok and set to a high heat.

FUNKY CHICKEN SANDWICH

There's nothing better for lunch than a hearty, healthy sandwich!

1 roll **Ciabatta** or 2 slices **sourdough**

3 Tbsp **Mango Mayonnaise** (see page 60)

Half a handful of **rocket**

¼ **cucumber** (6 slices) – shaved or sliced

80g **Funky BBQ Chicken** (see page 142) or **roasted chicken**

30g fresh or canned **mango** – sliced

1 tsp **toasted almonds**

1 tsp **Sweet Chilli Sauce** (see page 64)

Cut bread in half. Spread 1 tablespoon mango mayonnaise on each piece of bread. Use rocket to cover the base.

Fold cucumber slices in half and layer on top of rocket. Next add a layer of chicken. Add a layer of fresh or canned mango.

Place a dollop of mango mayonnaise on the top. Add almonds and drizzle with sweet chilli sauce. Place the bread top on and serve.

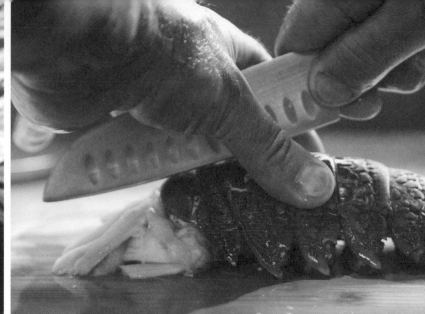

SEAFOOD DELICACIES

Full of omega-3 and omega-6 fatty acids, fish and seafood is one of the best foods we can eat to stay healthy inside and out. And it's tasty! And versatile. Fish and seafood can be used in curries, soups, grilled, fried, baked, steamed, the list goes on and on. Fresh is always best, and we're pretty lucky in New Zealand to be surrounded by great fishing waters. If you don't have an awesome local fishmonger or access to fresh fish, snap frozen is good too and maintains the good oils that seafood is full of.

SEAFOOD CHOWDER

It's chunky, filling, healthy, scrumptious, so good you'll want it every night! If you're a seafood fan, this will be the best darn chowder you've ever tasted! An oldie, a goodie, and definitely yummy!

200g **butter** – chopped

2 **shallots** – chopped

4 cloves **garlic** – peeled and chopped

180g **baby carrots** – chopped

½ **red capsicum/pepper** – sliced lengthways and then angle-sliced

½ **yellow capsicum/pepper** – sliced lengthways and then angle-sliced

200g short **celery sticks** – chopped

800g **potatoes** – peeled and diced

250g **firm fish** (we used hapuka) – chopped into chunks

10 **mussels** – cleaned and debearded

300g **scallops** – fresh or frozen

250g **prawns** – fresh or frozen

1L **fish stock**

1L **warm water**

1 tsp **turmeric**

Zest and **juice** of 1 **lemon**

400ml can **coconut milk**

3 Tbsp **arrowroot**

Salt and **pepper**

Parsley – to garnish

Heat a large pan over a medium-high heat. Add butter to pan with shallots and garlic. Take a moment to smell that amazing aroma!

Add carrots, capsicums, celery and potatoes to the pan. Sauté everything until softened.

Add fish, mussels (shells and all), scallops and prawns to the pan. Add fish stock and warm water. Add turmeric. Add lemon zest and juice and stir well.

Bring the mixture to a boil then reduce heat to medium and simmer for 30 minutes.

Add half the coconut milk. Pour the other half into a bowl and add the arrowroot. Whisk until smooth then add to the chowder.

Stir chowder until thick. Add salt and pepper to taste and garnish with parsely.

BBQ STUFFED FISH

Fresh fish – whether you caught it yourself or you bought it fresh from your local fishmonger or store – is so incredibly healthy and good for you. The omega-3 oils that are in all fish, more so in some, keep your bones, nails, hair and brain in good condition, like a well-oiled machine! But here's something you might not know – the smaller fish are actually better for you because they have less mercury in them. So next time you're choosing a fish for dinner, go for a few smaller ones rather than the biggest in the market!

1 whole **fish** (any type and fresh as!) – descaled and cleaned

1 whole **chilli** – chopped seeds and all

2 **limes** – 1 cut into fine wedges, 1 quartered

1 thumb **ginger** – chopped

1 Tbsp **coconut oil**

1 tsp **flaky salt**

TO SERVE

Green salad

Slice incisions into both sides of the fish and place a piece of chilli, fine lime wedge and ginger in each slot. Stuff the lime quarters and any remaining ginger into the body cavity.

Rub the fish with coconut oil and sprinkle with flaky salt.

Cook over BBQ embers, or very low flame, otherwise you'll burn your fish! Cook for about 7–10 minutes each side or until flesh

Serve with salad.

TIP – If you have my The Game Chef cookbook there's a great section on prepping all animals for cooking including fish...

15 min 15 min (crayfish)  Serves 2 NF

CRAYFISH SANDWICH

Oh, the tender sweetness of a fresh cray, cooked to perfection and sandwiched in scrumptiousness – yes please!

¾ loaf **ciabatta bread** – halved horizontally

30g **Chilli Butter** (See page 40)

50g **mascarpone cheese**

Handful of **baby rocket**

130g fresh cooked/boiled **crayfish meat**

50g **gruyère cheese** – sliced.

20g **butter**

1 clove **garlic** – crushed and chopped

Preheat the oven to 180°C.

Spread the top piece of bread with chilli butter. Spread the bottom piece of bread with mascarpone cheese.

Cover the base of the sandwich with baby rocket, add crayfish meat and top with gruyère cheese.

Place the sandwich base on a roasting/oven tray.

Place butter and garlic in a small hot pan and heat until butter is melted. Pour butter mixture over the sandwich fillings and then place in the oven for 8 minutes or until the cheese has melted. Top with the top piece of bread. Is your mouth watering – mine is!

GREEK FISH STEW

This is an awesome recipe if you have some firm fish such as trevally gurnard, kahawai, groper ('hapuka' in NZ), cod, hoki, carp, halibut, or haddock even. Ask your local fishmonger what firm fish is in season and is sustainably fished! Greek Fish Stew is a super tasty and hearty, wholesome recipe that really reminds me of the scents and flavours that are carried on the breeze in the Greek Isles.

3 Tbsp **extra virgin olive oil**

2 cloves **garlic** – crushed and chopped

1 **red onion** – sliced into rings

1 tsp **fresh rosemary**

1 Tbsp **oregano** – fresh or dried

1 Tbsp **capers**

Handful of **Kalamata olives**

1 cup chopped **celery** and **leaves**

2 medium-sized **potatoes** – scrubbed and diced

2 **carrots** – peeled and thickly sliced

400g can crushed **tomatoes**

1 **lemon** – zest and wedged

800ml **fish stock**

½ cup **white wine**

400g **fish** – cut into bite-size chunks

400g can **white beans**

Salt and **pepper**

TO SERVE

Chunky, freshly **baked bread**

Heat oil in a large saucepan over a high heat, add garlic and onions and fry until brown.

Add rosemary, oregano, capers, olives and celery and mix through. Add potatoes, carrots and tomatoes and stir to combine.

Add lemon zest then cut zested lemon into wedges, squeeze the juice into the pot and throw the lemon wedges into the mix. Add fish stock and white wine.

Bring the mixture to a boil then add fish and cook for 45 minutes. Add white beans and cook for a further 15 minutes.

Add salt and pepper to taste then serve in bowls with some chunky, freshly baked bread. Delicious!

30 min  20 min Serves 2–4 ⊗ NF

CRAYFISH CAESAR SALAD

This is my special take on the famous Caesar Salad invented by an Italian in Mexico! Crayfish is such a delicacy, and the meat of the tail is so tender, sweet, and juicy, I just had to include this scrumptious seafood in this cookbook. If you've ever had a fresh cray from the West Coast of the South Island, you'll know what I mean when I describe the flesh as sweet!

1 medium **crayfish** – preferably fresh!

4 rashers **streaky bacon** – chopped

3 Tbsp **olive oil**

1 tsp **fresh rosemary**

1 tsp **fresh thyme**

1 tsp **fresh oregano**

170g **French stick** or ½ loaf **ciabatta** – chopped into bite-sized pieces

Salt and **pepper**

1 medium-sized **cos lettuce**

2 Tbsp **powdered Parmesan cheese**, plus extra, grated, to serve

2½ Tbsp **Caesar Dressing** (see page 63)

2 **anchovies**

2 **boiled eggs** – cooled, shelled and cut lengthways

Preheat oven to 180°C.

Carefully drop the crayfish into a large pot of boiling water and cook for 15 minutes. Drain water. Twist off tail – gently! Use a fine, sharp knife to slice down centre of the back of the tail, cutting tail in half. Remove intestine – you'll see this on one of the cut sides – then peel off shell. Keep the tail end aside for presentation. Slice crayfish meat into bite-size pieces – refrigerate.

Fry bacon until crispy in a hot pan with 1 tablespoon oil until crispy. Set aside.

In a roasting dish add the remaining 2 tablespoons of olive oil, rosemary, thyme and oregano. Toss bread through. Sprinkle with salt and pepper. Bake for 5 minutes or until golden. Set aside.

Clean, dry and chop lettuce on an angle – leave smaller leaves whole. Place lettuce in a bowl. Toss through powdered Parmesan. Add 1 tablespoon Caesar dressing and mix.

Take crayfish from fridge and add 1 tablespoon Caesar dressing and mix through.

To serve, layer lettuce, serving spoon of crayfish, croutons, then bacon on large serving platter. Repeat until all the ingredients have been used. Drizzle remaining ½ tablespoon of Caesar dressing over the top. Place anchovies and the eggs artistically on the top. Sprinkle with grated Parmesan cheese, season with salt and pepper and serve.

PRAWN COCKTAIL SALAD

Handful of **iceberg lettuce** – thinly sliced

½ small **sweet red tomato** – sliced

1 **lemon**

Salt and **pepper**

80g **cooked prawns** – fresh or frozen

1 Tbsp **Aioli** or **Mayonnaise** (see page 62 and page 60)

1 Tbsp **Napoletana** Sauce (see page 50) or **tomato sauce**

Pinch of **paprika**

Toss the lettuce and tomato in a mixing bowl. Cut a wedge from the lemon and squeeze the juice from it over the salad.z Season with salt and pepper.

Keep 2 prawns with tails on for presentation. Remove the tails from the rest of the prawns and place in a bowl. Add aoili or mayonnaise and napoletana sauce and stir through.

Take an old-fashioned champagne glass (if you have one, otherwise use whatever vessel you would like). Make a nest with the salad then fill with the prawn cocktail mixture.

Slice the remainder of the lemon for presentation and to squeeze over the prawns. Sprinkle with smoked paprika. Garnish with the reserved prawn tails before serving.

20 min   15–20 min   Serves 1–2   DF   GF   NF

GREEK-STYLE STUFFED CALAMARI

I love this recipe because the texture of the calamari is just so good when done on a barbecue. Of course, you don't have to barbecue it, but I love the charred flavours you can achieve and barbecuing is about as close to wild cooking you can get!

2 Tbsp **extra virgin olive oil** plus extra for cooking

2 cloves **garlic** – crushed and roughly chopped

½ medium-sized **red onion** – sliced

½ **red capsicum/pepper** – sliced

Handful (about 12) of pitted **Kalamata olives**

1 **tomato** – finely chopped

Handful of **spinach leaves**

1 tsp freshly picked **oregano leaves**

Sprig of **Italian parsley leaves**

Zest and **juice** of ½ a **lemon**, plus extra juice for basting

¼ cup **white wine**

½ cup **breadcrumbs** – GF or standard

1 tsp **salt**

1 tsp **pepper**

3 **calamari tubes** – cleaned

Sprigs of **rosemary sprigs**

TO SERVE
Rocket leaves

Preheat a medium-sized pan. Heat 2 tablespoons olive oil, then add garlic, red onion, red capsicum, olives, tomato, spinach, oregano, parsley, lemon zest and juice. Stir well to combine.

Once the onions and the peppers are cooked or browned off, add white wine. Then add GF breadcrumbs, salt and pepper. Mix through until breadcrumbs absorb all the moisture.

Spoon the tomato mixture into the calamari tubes until full.

Lightly score the calamari but don't cut through on both sides. If you don't feel confident in scoring without cutting through don't do it! Just leave them unscored.

Brush the calamari with olive oil and sprinkle with salt and pepper on both sides before placing on the barbecue grill.

While on barbecue, squeeze lemon juice over and use the rosemary sprigs to baste. You can also add more oil if needed. Cook until charred then serve on a bed of rocket.

TIP – You can fry in a pan or oven bake if you don't feel like barbecuing.

PASTA, PIZZA PIZAZZ

Pizza is in my blood. My beautiful mother was a fantastic Italian cook and her pizza and pasta dough recipe should have been preserved for eternity in the Sistine Chapel. Although most Italians would say the same of their own Mama's dough! Though mine isn't quite the same as my mother's it's pretty close and my kids love it! Hopefully they go on in the future to tell their kids how nothing will ever compare to their Dad, *Angelo's Wild Kitchen* pizza!

 2 hrs 15 min   15 min    Makes 8 medium-sized pizzas   DF   NF   Ⓨ V

PIZZA DOUGH

Pizza is such a fun way to bring the family together. Share the prep, get the kids chopping ingredients – awesome fun!

Here I've included my own Pizza Dough from scratch and several of my family's favourite topping combos in the next page as an inspiration – but, as always, I implore you guys to get stuck in and invent your own too!

STARTER

25g **fresh yeast**

200ml **lukewarm water**

2 Tbsp **high-grade flour**

DOUGH

400g **flour**, plus extra for kneading

½ tsp **salt**

½ tsp **sugar**

STARTER

Mix yeast into water and add flour to make a paste. Set aside for 30 minutes.

DOUGH

On a clean bench mix the flour, salt and sugar with your fingers. Make a well in the centre and add the yeast mixture a bit at a time, mixing it into the flour as you go.

Once a dough has been formed, start kneading! Get the kids to each have a turn! You'll need to dust flour onto the bench to stop it sticking. Continue kneading for 10–15 minutes.

Place dough in a large bowl and cover with a damp tea towel. Place in a warm room – sometimes the car on a warm day is the perfect temperature – for 2 hours.

After 2 hours, place the dough on bench and roll into a thick sausage shape. Divide it evenly into 8 pieces. Each piece should be about 170g.

Roll each piece into a ball. Each ball makes one pizza base and you can roll out as thin or as thick as you like.

Cook the pizza at 180°C. How long you cook your pizza will depend on the toppings you choose – but the base should be raised and starting to golden.

Now let's get creative! And don't forget, it's all about having fun as a family – let the kids create their own! They're sure to eat it!

TOPPING INSPIRATION

EGGPLANT & SPINACH PIZZA

Napoletana Sauce (see page 50) – blended

Eggplant – cooked

Mozzarella cheese

Spinach

COUNTRY VEGETARIAN PIZZA

Napoletana Sauce (see page 50)

Mozzarella cheese – mixture of pre-shredded mozzarella, and real grated mozzarella

Field mushroom – sliced

Capsicum/pepper – sliced

Red onion – sliced into rings

Eggplant – sautéed

Courgette

Artichoke hearts

Onions

COURGETTE PROSCIUTTO PIZZA

Napoletana Sauce (see page 50)

Mozzarella – mixture of pre-shredded mozzarella, and real grated mozzarella

Prosciutto

Caramelised onions

Courgette – sliced

HARE & PLUM SAUCE PIZZA

Plum Sauce (See page 56)

Mozzarella – mixture of pre-shredded mozzarella, and real grated mozzarella

Hare – seared in a pan with oil and salt and pepper and sliced

Field mushroom – sliced

Fresh thyme

Fresh rosemary

COCONUT YOGHURT, BLACKBERRY PIZZA

Coconut yoghurt
Blackberry Sauce (See page 58)

SEAFOOD PIZZA

Napoletana Sauce (see page 50)
Classic Italian Pesto (see page 44) – plus extra to drizzle over the top
Mozzarella – mixture of pre-shredded mozzarella, and real grated mozzarella
Prawns (whole)
Smoked mussels – chopped
Artichoke hearts – pulled apart
Capsicum/pepper
Lemon juice – drizzled over the top

CHORIZO & EGPPLANT PIZZA

Chorizo – sliced or chopped
Eggplant – sliced or chopped
Caramelised onions

SMOKED MUSSEL PIZZA

Napoletana Sauce (see page 50)
Mozzarella – mixture of pre-shredded mozzarella, and real grated mozzarella
Smoked mussels – halved
Capsicum/pepper – sliced
Roast garlic oil – drizzled over the top

FETA, OLIVE & ANCHOVY PIZZA

Napoletana Sauce (see page 50)
Mozzarella – mixture of pre-shredded mozzarella, and real grated mozzarella
Goat's cheese feta – crumbled
Olives – black or green, pitted
Anchovies

SMOKED FISH & HALOUMI PIZZA

Napoletana Sauce (see page 50)
Mozzarella – mixture of pre-shredded mozzarella, and real grated mozzarella
Smoked fish – crumbled or chopped roughly
Haloumi – diced

GF GNOCCHI

Gnocchi is one of the most versatile dishes from Italy that I just love to play with, and by making it gluten free, everyone can enjoy this stunning, easy, filling and quick pasta. Gnocchi can be frozen and can be cooked from frozen, so it's a fantastic option to keep in the freezer for those last-minute meals.

1kg **Agria potatoes**

2 **egg yolks**

100g **standard GF flour**

75g **coconut flour**

75g **almond meal**

Peel potatoes, cut in half if big, and boil in a pot of water for 15 minutes, until half cooked then set aside to cool. Once cooled, grate the potatoes onto to a clean bench.

Mix egg yolks in a cup or bowl and then drizzle over potato and mix through.

Blend flours and almond meal together then mix into potato mixture on bench.

Dust bench with GF flour and shape/roll mixture into a long thin roll around 2cm in width. Chop into 1cm-width pieces. Roll off a fork to corrugate and shape. Place gently in a bowl.

Place in a large saucepan of boiling water for up to 10 minutes or until the gnocchi floats. Remove with a straining spoon and set aside.

Serve with the sauce of your choice or use in dishes such as my hare recipe on page 132

To freeze, place carefully in rows in a freezer bag and seal completely, removing as much air from the bag as possible. Lie flat in the freezer if possible while freezing.

15 min    20 min   Serves 6–8   ⊗ NF

CHORIZO RIGATONI

Pasta is a great way to feed a growing, hungry family. This particular recipe is a family favourite and will feed even me and my two boys! The chorizo adds a spicy tingle to the pasta, complementing the olives and feta to perfection.

650g **rigatoni**

2 Tbsp **extra virgin olive oil**

150g **chorizo sausage** – halved lengthways and then angle-sliced

4 cups **Napoletana Sauce** (see page 50)

1 cup **Kalamata olives**

TO SERVE

Fresh basil leaves

Feta cheese

Again, with all types of pasta everyone will have their opinion on how they prefer theirs cooked. Me, I like my pasta with a bit of substance – so I cook mine to a softly springy al dente.

Fill a large pot around three-quarters full of water and bring to the boil. Add rigatoni and let the water come to the boil again, then reduce heat and simmer for around 10 minutes or until you've taste-tested a piece as being al dente. Drain and set aside.

Place a large pan over high heat. Add oil.

Add chorizo and fry until golden. Once the sausages are starting to curl add napoletana sauce and simmer. Add olives and simmer for 4–6 minutes.

To serve you can either dish the pasta into each bowl and then distribute the topping OR toss it all together in the large saucepan – up to you!

Top with crumbled or chopped feta and fresh basil before serving.

 10 min 15–20 min 🍴 Serves 4

FETTUCCINE WITH CALAMARI, SICILIAN OLIVES, PESTO & ANGEL TOMATOES

This is a gorgeously healthy pasta dish with heavy Sicilian influence. Olives, calamari and tomato are also eaten in spades in the Greek Islands and are some of the reasons the Mediterranean people are known for their robust health and vigour – like me. ;)

250g **fettuccine**

200g **calamari** or **squid rings**

3 Tbsp **extra virgin olive oil**

2 cloves **garlic** – roughly chopped

Juice of ¼ a **lemon**

Handful (about 20) of **angel tomatoes**

4 Tbsp **Classic Italian Pesto** (see page 44)

12 large **sicilian olives**

Pepper to taste

TO SERVE

Fresh basil leaves

Fill a large pot around three-quarters full of water and bring to the boil. Add fettuccine and let the water come to the boil again, then reduce heat and simmer for around 10 minutes or until you've taste-tested a piece as being al dente. Drain and set aside.

Cut calamari into rings.

Heat a large pan over high heat and add 1 tablespoon olive oil and add garlic. Add the calamari. Add juice of one quarter lemon.

Add calamari, lemon juice, angel tomatoes and pesto. Mix through then remove pan from heat and add olives and pepper.

Add remaining 2 tablespoons of olive oil to drained pasta and toss through. Toss pasta and sauce together and top with basil before serving.

TIP – Always wash calamari before cooking. Once cut and washed, place on a paper towel to absorb moisture.

GF OPTION

Toss a large handful of rocket leaves with a tablespoon of olive oil, juice of ¼ a lemon, and a tablespoon of balsamic vinegar.

Serve calamari mixture on rocket.

PORK BELLY, MUSHROOM & SAGE ORECCHIETTE

Pork belly is one of those meats that works in so many amazing ways. I've used it in a variety of dishes and it really does give a dish a sweet, juicy, salty flavour. Wild pork belly is far less fatty than storebought, and the flavour of the meat is simply incredible. You can taste the very earth, the wildness of the sky and forest, in the meat. If you're lucky enough to bag a wild pig, try this recipe out on some of the belly – you'll thank me for it!

250g **pork belly**

2 Tbsp **olive oil**

150g **white mushrooms** – sliced

2 cloves **garlic** – crushed and roughly chopped

½ tsp **salt**

½ tsp **ground black pepper**

1 Tbsp **sage** – chopped

4 **cherry tomatoes** –halved

250ml **cream**

3 Tbsp **white wine**

250g **oreecchiette**

1 **egg yolk**

¼ cup **grated** or **powdered Parmesan**

TO SERVE

Parmesan cheese

Slice the pork belly into 4 long slices and then chop into bite-size cubes.

Heat a large pan over high heat. Add olive oil. Get the pan hot – drop the pork in and fry until crispy – now this is important – not a hard, crunchy kind of crispy but just so the fatty end is golden and crisped.

Add mushrooms and garlic to the pork. Season with salt and pepper. Add sage and cherry tomatoes. Add cream and bring to a simmer, then add wine.

As soon as you add the cream get your orecchiette pasta on! Fill a large pot around three-quarters full of water and bring to the boil. Cover, ready to cook the oreecchiette for around 10 minutes or until al dente. Drain and set aside.

To the cream mix, add the egg yolk and stir through. Make sure you stir it right around the whole pan – you'll find the cream will thicken quite quickly as you stir it round. Add Parmesan and stir through. Take off heat. Add more salt and pepper to taste.

Toss drained orecchiette through sauce through sauce and serve with as much additional Parmesan as you like.

WILD ASIAN FUSION

While Steph and I were in Chiang Mai, we discovered more than just a new way to cook - we discovered a new way to think about cooking. I've always cooked by taste, what I know will work together, what I imagine might work together, but in Thailand I learned to cook by feel. What foods felt right together, the rightness of how we gathered and foraged for our ingredients, and where they came from. Asian fusion aligns perfectly with my Wild Kitchen philosophy, as the basis of most Asian countries' cuisines is to eat what's local, what they gather, what's in season, and has been for thousands of years. And the flavours are just outstanding!

STEAMED BUNS

My first restaurant job was working in a Chinese restaurant in London. It was there I discovered the epicurean beauty of a freshly steamed bun. A great way to use leftover cooked meat! Of course, you can use fresh meat for this and cook from raw.

BUN

500g **high-grade self-raising flour**

½ tsp **yeast**

½ tsp **salt**

400ml **warm water**

TO COOK

Rice bran oil

Place flour into a bowl. Mix yeast and salt with water, then add to flour. Work through or knead for 10 minutes. Place dough in a bowl, cover with a damp tea towel and let it rest for 40 minutes somewhere warm.

Once dough has risen, roll out into a long sausage shape around 4cm in diameter. Cut in half and halve and halve again until you end up with 16 pieces. Roll pieces into round balls. They should weigh around 60g each.

Use a little bit of flour for dusting a clean workbench.

Dust rolling pin. Roll each ball out flat into a mini pizza base with thinner edges and thicker centre.

Place 1 heaped tablespoon of mixture (the choice of filling is yours, see following pages) in the middle. Create little 'money bag' pouches, squeezing the dough together at the top until sealed. Turn over and round into smooth buns with your hands.

In a small wok add some water to just over halfway and place the steamer on top. Cut 16 x 70mm squares of baking paper. Place in the bottom of a bamboo steamer so that buns don't stick to steamer. Place buns on paper, brush with rice bran oil.

Steam for 15 minutes. Depending on size of your steamer and wok you might have to do this in 2 or 4 batches.

STEAMED BUN FILLINGS

I've put together some of my favourite fillings for steamed buns. The following recipes can be used for lunches, the evening meal, or even breakfast! There's no rules on when to eat a steamed bun! Prep your dough first, then choose one of the fillings below.

 15–30 min   15 min/batch    Makes 16   DF   NF

STEAMED BREAKFAST BUNS

2 Tbsp **rice bran oil,** plus extra for brushing

1 Tbsp **sesame oil**

4 rashers **bacon** – thinly sliced

2 cloves **garlic** – finely chopped

1 cup finely shredded **cabbage**

60g **red capsicum/pepper**

2 **mushrooms** – finely chopped

2 Tbsp **soy sauce**

2 Tbsp **Sweet Chilli Sauce** (see page 64)

½ cup **black beans** – canned or precooked fresh

4 **boiled eggs** – peeled and quartered

Heat rice bran and sesame oil in a wok over high heat. In goes the bacon and garlic. Once browned off, add cabbage, capsicum and mushroom and stir-fry through. Add soy sauce, sweet chilli sauce, and stir through then removed from heat.

Stir through black beans.

Place 1 heaped tablespoon of mixture into the centre of each piece of the rolled bun dough (see page 106). Place half an egg on top of mixture. Wrap in a money bag, seal and shape then place in the steamer.

Brush with oil, cover and steam for 15 minutes.

 15–30 min 15 min/batch  Makes 16 DF NF

CHICKEN, MANGO
& BOK CHOY STEAMED BUNS

2 Tbsp **rice bran oil**

2 cloves **garlic** – finely chopped

1 thumb **ginger** – finely chopped

1 Tbsp **sesame oil**

2 Tbsp **Sweet Chilli Sauce** (see page 64)

120g **chicken** – cooked or uncooked, works both ways

130g **bok choy** – finely chopped

1 Tbsp **soy sauce**

1 Tbsp **fish sauce**

1 tsp **arrowroot**

2 Tbsp **water**

120g sliced **mango** – canned or fresh

Heat rice bran and sesame oil in a wok over a high heat. Add garlic, ginger and sweet chilli sauce. Add chicken and stir-fry until chicken is cooked. Add bok choy and stir-fry. Add soy sauce and fish sauce, stir-fry for another 30 seconds and then place in a bowl.

Mix arrowroot with water and add to the stir-fry mix to thicken filling mixture.

Place 1 heaped tablespoon of mixture in the centre of each piece of the rolled-out bun dough (see page 106). Place a slice of mango on top of mixture.

Wrap in a money bag, seal and shape then place in the steamer.

Brush with oil, cover and steam for 15 minutes.

 15–30 min 15 min/batch  Makes 16 DF NF V

BANANA & BLACK BEAN FRIED BUNS

2 Tbsp **rice bran oil**

½ x 400g tin **black beans**

2 **bananas**

3 Tbsp **coconut sugar**

½ tsp **vanilla essence**

½ tsp **ground ginger**

½ cup **canola oil** or **vegetable oil**, plus extra for steaming

TO SERVE

Coconut yoghurt or mascarpone (optional)

2 tsp coconut sugar

½ tsp cinnamon

Heat rice bran oil in a wok over medium heat. Add black beans, sliced bananas, coconut sugar, vanilla essence and ginger. Cook until bananas are soft and golden looking.

Place 1 heaped tablespoon of mixture in the centre of each piece of the rolled-out bun dough (see page 106). Add a dollop of coconut yoghurt or mascarpone if you like.

Wrap in a money bag, seal and shape then place in the steamer. Brush with oil, cover and steam for 15 minutes.

Once steamed, place the buns in a hot pan or wok with canola or vegetable and fry for 1 minute on each side or until golden brown.

Sprinkle with coconut sugar and cinnamon, and serve with coconut yoghurt, if desired.

PORK & CHILLI CABBAGE STEAMED BUNS

Yummy, easy, light, and filling, this gorgeous Asian fusion dish will become a fast favourite. All the flavours are here that makes Asian-styled food so delicious. Do me a favour and take a good sniff of the sesame oil – the aroma is simply divine!

2 Tbsp **rice bran oil**

1 Tbsp **sesame oil**

2 cloves **garlic** – finely chopped

1 thumb **ginger** – finely chopped

2 medium **white mushrooms** – finely chopped

200g **cabbage** – finely chopped

100g **leftover roast** or **pre-cooked pork** – diced

2 Tbsp **hoisin sauce**

2 Tbsp **black bean sauce**

1 Tbsp **Sweet Chilli Sauce** (see page 64)

TO SERVE

Black sesame seeds

Fresh coriander – chopped

Spring onions

Hoisin sauce

Bean sprouts

Heat rice bran oil and sesame oil in a wok over high heat.

Add garlic, ginger, mushrooms and cabbage and pork to wok. Stir-fry for 1–2 minutes.

Add hoisin and black bean sauces. Stir-fry for another minute.

Take off the heat and place into a bowl. Add sweet chilli sauce and stir through.

Place 1 heaped tablespoon of mixture in the centre of each piece of the rolled-out bun dough (see page 106).

Wrap in a money bag, seal and shape then place in the steamer.

Brush with oil, cover and steam for 15 minutes.

Sprinkle with black sesame seeds. Serve with coriander, spring onions, bean sprouts and hoisin sauce for dipping.

ASIAN-STYLE SOUP

Soup is such a staple in Asia. They literally throw anything they can forage into a big pot with spices and water and create the most delectable soups I've ever tasted. This is a pretty simple soup, but trust me, it's really good and it fills you up in a healthy way!

1 Tbsp **rice bran oil**

1 tsp **sesame seed oil**

1 clove **garlic** – chopped

6g **fresh ginger** – thinly sliced

10 medium **white mushrooms** – thinly sliced

100g **chicken breast** – sliced into strips

½ **red chilli** – thinly sliced

1L **chicken stock**

1 cup thinly sliced **cabbage**

GARNISH

Handful of **mung beans**

Spring onion

Pinch of **black sesame seeds**

Boiled egg

Coriander

Slice chicken breast into strips.

Preheat wok and add both rice bran and sesame oils. Add garlic, ginger, and chilli to wok and stir-fry for 1 minute. Add mushrooms and chicken and stir-fry for 4 minutes, then add chicken stock.

Add cabbage and simmer for 10 minutes.

Ladle into serving bowls and garnish with mung beans, spring onions, boiled egg, coriander and black sesame seeds.

GIVE ME GREENS

We all know how good our greens are for our bodies, but do you know how good they are for your mind and your soul? Vegetables, eaten in season, raw or cooked, provide us with the right nutrients and minerals we need to function at our best. Fruit and vegetables grow in certain regions in certain seasons for a good reason – because they help our system cope with the environment. In winter we need vitamin C to fight colds and flus, so nature grows us orange fruits and veges. Nature is an amazing thing and knows what we need better than we do. It pays to listen.

ANGELO'S GREEK SALAD

Salads can be as filling as you want them to be. If there's one thing I've discovered in the last year of getting my body and mind healthy, it's that a salad is a meal, not just a side. I love sitting down to a good, big salad now, full of amazing tastes and flavours from Greece, the pep of chilli, the creamy salt of feta, the fresh tang of vine-ripened tomatoes – oh yum, is it time for lunch yet?

3 **lebanese cucumbers**

5 vine-ripened **tomatoes**

¼ **red onion**

2 Tbsp **extra virgin olive oil**

½ **red capsicum/pepper** – sliced

Pinch of **chilli flakes**

Pinch of **lemon pepper**

½ tsp **fennel seeds**

½ tsp **coriander seeds** (crushed with mortar and pestle)

120g **feta cheese** – chopped into 1cm cubes

Pinch of **turmeric**

½ cup **Kalamata olives**

1 Tbsp **avocado oil**

Juice of ½ a **lemon**

½ Tbsp **fresh rosemary** – chopped

½ Tbsp **fresh thyme** – chopped

Salt and **pepper**

TO SERVE

1 tsp **flat-leaf parsley** – chopped

Avocado oil

Extra virgin olive oil

Slice cucumbers very thinly lengthways and then into thirds on an angle. Use a mandolin slicer if you have one. Set aside in a bowl.

Cut tomatoes into 10 wedges. You want these to be so small and cute rather than big and chunky. Place these sweet babies in bowl with cucumber.

Slice onion into thin onion rings. Add to cucumber and tomato in bowl.

Heat a medium saucepan over high heat. Add 1 tablespoon of extra virgin olive oil. Add capsicum, chilli flakes, lemon pepper, fennel seeds and coriander seeds. Toss through, making sure capsicum is coated and then place in a separate bowl and let cool. Watch those coriander seeds, they do like to dance!

Using the same pan that was used for capsicum, add feta and toss until coated in oil. Once coated, sprinkle with turmeric. Set aside in a dish to cool.

Add olives and cooled capsicums to the cucumber mixture. Add avocado oil, remaining extra virgin olive oil and lemon juice.

Sprinkle with rosemary and thyme, salt and pepper. Toss salad gently using hands.

Serve in a salad bowl and sprinkle with parsley. Drizzle with avocado oil and extra olive oil before serving.

TIP – You don't want to cook the feta cheese for more than 30 seconds, it's just a flash in the pan to coat in oil and warm through.

ANNA'S EGGPLANT PARMIGIANA

My Mama, Anna, used to make this dish and I just love it so much! It will keep in the fridge for up to 6 days and still tastes great! By slightly dehydrating the eggplant you end up with a better consistency in the dish. This is definitely one of the kids' faves and was a sell-out dish at my old café in Auckland, The Fridge. And it's so darn simple!

1.3kg **eggplants**

4 Tbsp **olive oil**

300ml **Napoletan**a Sauce (see page 50)

200–300g **Parmesan** – sliced and extra grated Parmesan cheese for topping

Pepper

Preheat the oven to 180°C.

Slice the eggplant lengthways into thin slices. Lay slices on a clean tea towel and sprinkle with salt. Leave for 10 minutes. The salt will draw the moisture from the eggplant, giving the flesh a slight dehydrated texture. Repeat on the other side. Use paper towels to draw out/mop up any excess moisture.

Pour the olive oil in a large pan. Brown off both sides of the eggplant slices, then place in a bowl. Reapply olive oil between batches of eggplant.

Coat the bottom of an ovenproof dish with napoletana sauce , then a layer of eggplant, then a layer of Parmesan cheese slices then repeat, repeat, repeat until you get to the top and then you finish with grated Parmesan and pepper.

Bake in the oven for 20 minutes or until Parmesan has "browned off."

One healthy, yummy, easy dish ready to serve!

SUPER-DUPER WOK-FRIED VEGES

Great for vegetarians and as a side dish with barbecued meat, or for lunch, Super-Duper Wok-Fried Veges have a super flavour and are incredibly healthy and delicious. You can use frozen or fresh veges – always best from your own garden! My son, Luca, has an amazing vege garden and he loves picking what I need for dinner from it. I'm super proud! Can you tell?

3 Tbsp **rice bran oil**

4 cloves **garlic** – crushed and chopped

30g fresh **ginger** – sliced into long pieces

1 whole **red onion** – thinly sliced lengthways

1 **chilli** – deseeded and finely chopped

1 stalk **lemongrass** – thinly angle-sliced

1 **red capsicum/pepper** – sliced lengthways

4 **carrots** – peeled, halved lengthways and angle-sliced

1 Tbsp **sesame seed oil**

4 **courgettes** – halved lengthways and angle-sliced

1.5 heads **bok choy** – cleaned, each leaf angle-sliced into three pieces

1 Tbsp **fish sauce**

4 Tbsp **black bean sauce**

4 Tbsp **hoisin sauce**

2 Tbsp **soy sauce**

4 medium-sized **mushrooms** – thinly sliced

1 heaped Tbsp **black sesame seeds**

TO SERVE

Fresh coriander – chopped

Spring onions – chopped

Mung beans

Hoisin sauce

Heat rice bran oil in a large wok.

Garlic, ginger, onions, chilli and lemongrass go in first.

Next add the red capsicum/pepper. Stir quickly.

Add carrots and toss through.

Add sesame oil.

Now add the courgettes and bok choy.

Add fish sauce.

Add black bean sauce, hoisin sauce and soy sauce.

Then add mushrooms and black sesame seeds.

Serve with coriander, spring onions, mung beans and hoisin sauce for dipping.

TIP –Get the wok really hot before you add the oil and then add the veges quickly. And leaves seeds in chilli if you want more heat.

BBQ SWEETCORN WITH CHILLI BUTTER & PARMESAN

This is a great way to barbecue corn and it tastes absolutely delicious! Corn is a staple ingredient in many countries and is used in a variety of ways. It's amazingly sweet and kids just love it!

75g **Chilli Butter** (see page 40) – softened

5 **corn cobs**

TO SERVE

Salt and **pepper**

Handful of grated **Parmesan**

Coat each cob with the chilli butter.

Place on barbecue grill and cook until slightly charred.

Take off the barbecue grill and sprinkle with salt, pepper and grated Parmesan.

Serve immediately.

MANGO, WATERMELON & AVOCADO SUMMER SALAD

Another great refreshing summery salad. Avocado provides you with the good fats your body needs, and the cooling, peppy flavours of the mint cleans and energises, while the sweetness of the watermelon and mango complements the intense tart–sweet pomegranate molasses. It's all just a bit of fantastic really.

1 **mango**

2 **avocados**

½ **watermelon**

Handful of **mint** or **spearmint**

3 Tbsp **avocado oil**

1 Tbsp **pomegranate molasses**

Salt and **pepper**

Cut all the fruit into bite-size pieces and place in a bowl.

Slice mint leaves. Sprinkle half of the mint leaves into the salad and toss through.

Mix avocado oil and pomegranate molasses together. Drizzle over salad. Add a pinch of salt and pepper.

Plate and sprinkle with the rest of the chopped mint leaves.

CAULIFLOWER CHEESE & VINE TOMATO BAKE

Usually when you hear 'bake' you think of the classic potato bake, which is a really good dish and super yummy and hearty. This is my twist on a bake and I think you're going to love it. Full of fresh vege and cheesy goodness, this bake utilises the amazing textures and versatility of cauliflower. Cauliflower is a truly epic vegetable and can be puréed, mashed, roasted, baked, steamed or stir-fried to create any number of stunning dishes.

8 **vine tomatoes**

3 Tbsp **olive oil**

1 tsp **fennel seeds**

Salt and pepper

½ head **cauliflower**

1 Tbsp **butter**

2 cloves **garlic** – roughly chopped

4 rashers **streaky bacon** – chopped into 2cm pieces

CHEESE SAUCE

2 cups **whole milk**

150g grated **cheddar cheese**

1 tsp **turmeric**

2 tsp **arrowroot** or **cornflour**

3 Tbsp **water**

Salt and **pepper**

TO SERVE

½ tsp **smoked paprika**

3 Tbsp GF **breadcrumbs**

3 Tbsp **pine nuts**

Preheat the oven to 180°C.

Place the vine tomatoes in an ovenproof dish. Drizzle with olive oil, sprinkle with fennel seeds and a pinch of salt and pepper. Bake in oven for 15 minutes. Take out and leave aside. Leave oven on.

Chop cauliflower into bite-size pieces. Add to a medium-sized pot of boiling water. Cook until softened, around 3–5 minutes, then drain well.

Heat medium-sized frying pan, add butter, garlic and bacon. Fry until golden brown.

Slowly heat the milk in another medium pot. Add cheese and turmeric. Stir constantly with a wooden spoon until cheese has melted.

Mix arrowroot or cornflour with water then add to cheese sauce. Add a pinch of black pepper and salt. Continue to stir sauce until thick.

Add cauliflower to bacon, garlic and butter mix. Toss through. Add mixture to an ovenproof dish.

Pour cheese mixture over the cauliflower mix, make sure you cover the cauliflower.

Place roasted vine tomatoes on top of cauliflower and sprinkle with smoked paprika, GF breadcrumbs and pine nuts. Roast in oven for 8 minutes.

Serve as a main on it's own, or as a side.

WARM SPINACH, FETA & BRUSSELS SPROUT SALAD

The humble brussels sprout has been given a bit of bad press over the years, but this little vege, which I like to think of as a condensed cabbage, is full of wholesome goodness and with the right companion cooking, is absolutely delish!

500ml **water**

Salt

20 **brussels sprouts** – trimmed

Knob of **butter** (roughly a teaspoon or maybe 2, you'll know!)

1 clove **garlic**

DRESSING

Handful of **spinach** (4 small spinach plants or frozen will work too)

150g **feta** – crumbled

1 tsp **cumin seeds**

Pepper

2 Tbsp **extra virgin olive oil**

3 Tbsp **Greek yoghurt**

Juice of ½ a **lemon**

2 Tbsp **powdered Parmesan cheese**

1 Tbsp **grated Parmesan cheese**

Preheat oven to 180°C.

Heat water in a medium-size pot and add a pinch of salt. Cook brussels sprouts in boiling water for 15 minutes. While the brussels sprouts are boiling, heat an ovenproof pan on the stove.

Add the butter and garlic to pan. Drain brussels sprouts and add to the pan. Toss until coated with butter and garlic then pop into oven for 10 minutes.

Remove stalks from spinach and add to blender with feta, cumin seeds, a pinch of pepper, olive oil, yoghurt and lemon juice. Blend for 40 seconds until it has a dip-like consistency.

Transfer brussels sprouts to bowl. Spoon dressing over sprouts and toss/mix through.

Mix in the powdered Parmesan.

Garnish with grated Parmesan and serve these fantastically tasty brussels sprouts!

MEAT

What can I say about meat? Too much, really. And I could certainly get a bit preachy about where it comes from, how it's handled and treated, and why it should be a heck of a lot cheaper so more people have easy access to lean, free-farmed or wild meats that have been raised or lived wild in stress-free environments. Beef, lamb, venison, goat, pork, and any other kind of farmed or wild animal should be treated with respect and dignity and we should feel thankful to and for them. Lean, fresh, stress-free meat is so good for our body, our brains, and if we are eating in clear conscience, our souls too. Full of protein and iron and a multitude of other healthy goodness, meat has been a human staple for centuries. It deserves respect – and a bloody good recipe.

HARE WITH BUTTER & SAGE GNOCCHI & PLUM SAUCE

100g **hare back straps**

Salt and **pepper**

400g **Gnocchi** (see page 96)

40g **butter**

2 cloves **garlic** – peeled and finely chopped

6 **sage leaves** – halved lengthways

½ tsp **rosemary,** plus extra to sprinkle

½ tsp **thyme,** plus extra to sprinkle

1 Tbsp **olive oil**

1 Tbsp **Plum Sauce** (see page 56), plus extra to serve

Prepare hare back straps. Remove as much of the shiny sinew as you can. Some people like to salt their hare to 'tenderise' it, or soak it in saline, but I leave mine as is. Just roll them in some plastic wrap and set aside.

Fill a large pan with water and bring to the boil. Add a pinch of salt. Place gnocchi in water and boil for around 10 minutes or until gnocchi floats.

Heat a frying pan over a high heat and add butter, garlic and sage leaves. Add rosemary and thyme. Sing the song… "Are you going to Scarborough Fair…"

As soon as the butter starts to turn a nutty brown colour add the gnocchi and toss through.

Heat a frying pan and drizzle in the olive oil. Place back straps into pan and sear, being careful not to overcook or to burn. Season both sides with salt and pepper while searing. Sprinkle with rosemary and thyme.

Coat straps with plum sauce. Take off heat and let rest for 2 minutes, then angle-slice into 1.5cm-thick slices.

Layer over the gnocchi and add some more plum sauce – just because you can!

RIB EYE STEAK WITH CREAMY MUSHROOM SAUCE & COURGETTES

Simple, scrumptious and a great and healthy way to eat steak.

170–225g **rib eye steak**

2 Tbsp **extra virgin olive oil**

Salt and **pepper**

1 small **courgette** – sliced lengthways

2 whole **vine ripened tomatoes**

1 large gourmet **mushroom**

1 Tbsp **butter**

Creamy Mushroom Sauce (see page 52)

Brush steak with oil on both sides and season with salt and pepper. Place on hot barbecue grill and cook until desired. Cover and set aside to rest.

While steak is on barbecue grill, brush courgette slices, tomatoes and mushrooms with oil. Place on barbecue grill and top with small chips of butter, salt and pepper. Veges should be done by the time steak has rested for 5 minutes.

Dish up and enjoy the simple pleasures of the mighty Kiwi barbecue!

Serve with Creamy Mushroom Sauce.

BBQ FLINTSTONE STEAK WITH MASCARPONE CREAMY SPINACH

Everyone loves a decent steak – okay, not everyone, but I do! You can use venison steaks or fillet for this dish as well. Steaks, especially fillet, are at their very best when cooked medium-rare. To make sure you get a good medium-rare steak, squeeze your hand into a fist and press your finger on the mound it makes near your thumb. A tight fist is well done – a loose fist is rare – guess where medium-rare is?

2 Tbsp **extra virgin olive oil**

2 cloves **garlic** – crushed and chopped

100g **spinach leaves** – stalks removed

100g **mascarpone cheese**

Salt and **pepper**

Pinch of **turmeric**

Pinch of **ground coriander**

100g **eye fillet**

1 **red capsicum/pepper**

1 Tbsp **olive oil**

Heat a large pan on the stove until a drop of water dances. Add extra virgin olive oil to pan and brown the garlic. Add spinach and toss.

Once spinach has wilted, reduce heat to medium, add mascarpone cheese and mix through. Add a pinch of salt and pepper. Add turmeric and ground coriander and mix through.

Brush steak and capsicum with olive oil on both sides. Season steak with salt and pepper on both sides. Place on barbecue grill and cook steak until medium-rare (or whatever you prefer).

Serve the mascarpone creamy spinach with the barbecued steak and capsicum. Voila!

TIP – Lay your meat out in the kitchen on a chopping board or platter until it's at room temperature. This helps the meat soften and cook without too much shrinkage.

STICKY BBQ PORK RIBS

Get out the bibs – it's time for ribs!

700g **pork spare ribs**

1 Tbsp **extra virgin olive oil**

½ tsp **Himalayan salt**

½ tsp **black pepper**

1 cup **BBQ Sauce** (see page 54)

Coat the pork ribs in the oil. Sprinkle salt and pepper over the top. Leave to sit while the barbecue grill heats up.

When barbecue grill is nice and hot, place ribs on grill. Turn regularly to cook nice and evenly through for 10 minutes.

When cooked through, place ribs into a shallow dish and coat with my delicious BBQ sauce. Make sure all the ribs are covered, then serve hot!

YUM!

VENISON WITH BLACKBERRY SAUCE & ROAST BEETROOT

Cook the venison to your liking – me, personally, I love mine medium-rare. If the skillet pan dries out, just add more oil. Oh, and yes, you can use a good cut of beef steak for this recipe as well! I like a nice, thick eye fillet!

200g **beetroot** – chopped

1 **shallot** – halved and sliced

1 clove **garlic** – chopped

2 Tbsp **olive oil**

1 Tbsp **balsamic vinegar**

Zest of ½ an **orange**

Salt and **pepper**

2 Tbsp **canola** or **vegetable oil**

500g **venison leg** or **rump** (or a whole eye fillet, scotch fillet, or rump of beef)

TO SERVE

Blackberry Sauce (see page 58)

Preheat oven to 190°C.

Place the beetroot, shallot and garlic into an ovenproof pan. Coat with olive oil and fry for two minutes.

Add balsamic vinegar, orange zest, and a pinch of salt and pepper. Give it all a bit of a mix to make sure the beetroot is coated.

Bake in oven for 12 minutes.

Put a skillet pan on the barbecue grill or stove and add canola or vegetable oil. Season meat with salt and pepper.

Add meat to pan and sear on both sides. Once cooked to your liking, let the meat rest for a few minutes. Pour any run off from the meat into the beetroot mix.

Slice the meat to the thickness you prefer – I like mine sliced thinly so it folds and drapes like flower petals. Warm blackberry sauce in a small saucepan, then drizzle over top and serve with the roast beetroot.

Beetroot is so good for you! It's absolutely jam packed with wholesome, healthy and hearty goodness! The more beetroot in your diet, the better. And it's great because you can eat it raw, roasted, baked, as a soup, as a mash or purée – it's just so versatile and tasty.

5–10 min   20–30 min    Serves 4   GF   NF

FUNKY BBQ CHICKEN

Super simple and made with my Spicy Herb Butter, let's all do the Funky Chicken!

1 **chicken** (any size)

2 Tbsp **olive oil**

2 Tbsp **Sweet Chilli Sauce** (see page 64)

Spicy Herb Butter (see page 42)

Cut the chicken right down the breastplate until you hit the backbone. Place chicken in a large bowl or dish. Coat chicken in oil.

Add sweet chilli sauce and coat the chicken.

Heat the barbecue, and when it's nice and hot, place the funky chicken on the grill. Once chicken is golden brown start brushing with spicy herb butter regularly until cooked.

ROAST PORK WITH PINEAPPLE

If you have wild pork, fantastic, if not, head to your local butcher and ask for free range pork. Stress-free food tastes better and anything that has grown up in a cage is bound to be stressed out. Free-farmed pork, poultry, beef and lamb is the way to go if you don't have access to wild meat.

2.5-3kg **pork leg**

8 cloves **garlic** – peeled

16 **sage leaves**

600g **fresh pineapple**

4 Tbsp **rice bran oil**

Himalayan salt and **pepper**

3 sprigs **sage**

Preheat the oven to 170°C.

Use a small prepping knife and cut slits into pork, 5-7cm deep and 5cm long.

Halve garlic cloves, wrap each half with a sage leaf and stuff into slits in pork.

Cut pineapple into 3 x 1-2cm rings and then quarter the rings – leave the skin on.

Coat the bottom of a roasting dish with 2 tablespoons rice bran oil, salt and pepper. Lay three sprigs of sage in the oil then place the pineapple on top of sage and pork on top of pineapple.

Pour remaining 2 tablespoons oil over the top and brush on so the pork is coated in oil. Use a coarse pepper and salt and thickly sprinkle over the top of the pork.

Bake in preheated oven for 90 minutes.

It's a little bit like a traditional Kiwi Christmas ham, but in my opinion, much tastier! The pineapple enhances the natural flavours in the pork. Serve with roast potatoes, black rice, or whatever you like!

STUFFED CHICKEN WITH PINEAPPLE AND PRAWNS

This bad boy chicken dish is full of flavour and surprising textures and is fantastic served with chunky, rustic roasted veges such as kumara, pumpkin, and parsnip. I use quite a lot of turmeric in my recipes – you might have noticed – as turmeric is so good for you. It has anti-inflammatory properties, anti-depressant properties, anti-coagulant properties, relieves pain, acts as a steroid – it's basically a medicinal miracle!

1 whole **chicken** (size 18–20)

STUFFING

2 cloves **garlic**

½ **onion** – sliced

½ tsp **turmeric**

1 tsp **lemon pepper**

120g fresh or canned **pineapple** – cut into 1cm cubes

1 whole **chilli** – sliced (seeds and all, depending on taste)

2 Tbsp **avocado oil**

1 Tbsp real **maple syrup**

1 tsp **wholegrain mustard**

½ cup **white wine**

150g **prawns** – tails removed

1 tsp **salt**

1 tsp **black pepper**

1 cup **GF breadcrumbs**

COATING

2 Tbsp **olive oil**

½ tsp **salt**

½ tsp **pepper**

½ tsp **turmeric**

Preheat oven to 200°C.

Place garlic, onion, turmeric, lemon pepper, pineapple and chilli in a mixing bowl.

Heat avocado oil in pan, add pineapple mixture and stir. Add maple syrup to caramelise the mixture. Add wholegrain mustard and stir through.

Add the white wine once the onions and pineapple have caramelised. Before the wine evaporates add the prawns to the mix and stir in. Add salt and pepper. Add GF breadcrumbs. Stir then take off heat and let the breadcrumbs absorb all the moisture.

Transfer stuffing mixture into a bowl and let cool before stuffing the chicken so you don't burn yourself!

Stuff the chicken. Make sure you push the stuffing mixture right in – don't be shy.

Cover the base of an oven dish with oil, salt and pepper and a dusting of turmeric. Place chicken in dish and then roll over so coated in oil mixture. Leave chicken tits-up (breast up).

Roast in oven for 40 minutes.

SAUTÉED CHICKEN LIVERS WITH MARSALA & SHALLOTS

Liver is incredibly high in protein and folate, which is vital for optimum fertility health – and not just for the ladies! Men need folate too to give our wee guys a fighting chance at creating perfect, beautiful life. Plus it's just bloody delicious!

2 Tbsp **olive oil**

2 cloves **garlic** – sliced lengthways

2 **shallots** – halved and sliced

1 Tbsp **soft brown sugar**

400g **chicken livers**

1 tsp **rosemary**

1 tsp **thyme**

½ cup **marsala** or **red wine**

2 sprigs of **fresh lavender**

200ml **cream**

½ tsp **salt**

1 tsp **black pepper**

100g **gruyère cheese**

Half a loaf **ciabatta bread** – sliced and lightly toasted

Heat olive oil in a large pan over a high heat. Add garlic and shallots and sauté.

Add the soft brown sugar to caramelise onions. Add chicken livers. Add rosemary and thyme. Cook livers on both sides.

Add marsala or red wine and sprigs of lavender. Cook until the marsala has evaporated then add cream.

Add salt and pepper then simmer over high heat for 3–5 minutes or until a thick sauce has been created.

Cut cheese into 6 slices or the right amount to match the number of livers. Place a slice of cheese onto each piece of liver. Pop into a hot oven or under a grill to melt the cheese.

Serve livers on toasted ciabatta.

NORTH AFRICAN BBQ GOAT HOTPOT WITH COCONUT YOGHURT

Goat curry is one of my personal favourite dishes. Goat has such a gorgeous flavour. It's gamey in a good way, and combined with made-from-scratch curry, it's just divine. It's also a super lean meat with hardly any fat, but retains a tender texture.

5 clove **garlic** – crushed and chopped

2 **onions** – chopped

1 whole **chilli** – chopped

20g **ginger** – chopped

3 Tbsp **olive oil**

2 small (1.5kg) **goat legs** – with bone

1 tsp **turmeric**

1 tsp **ground cumin**

1 tsp **fennel seeds**

1 tsp **garam masala**

6 **cloves**

1 tsp **smoked paprika**

1 tsp **cinnamon**

1 tsp **sumac**

Salt and **pepper**

1½ **lemon**

4 **ripe tomatoes**

Handful of chopped **celery sticks** and **leaves**

Handful of **fresh coriander** – finely chopped

2 x 400g tins whole or chopped **tomatoes**

1 glass of **red wine** (and an extra one for drinking)

300ml **beef stock**

Water

TO SERVE
Wild rice

Preheat the oven to 160°C.

Put 1 tablespoon oil, garlic, onion, chilli and ginger into a roasting dish.

Rub 2 tablespoons of olive oil into goat legs.

Combine turmeric, cumin, fennel seeds, garam masala, cloves, smoked paprika, cinnamon and sumac in a small bowl and sprinkle over the goat legs. Add a pinch of salt and pepper. Rub all spices and oil into the legs.

Place on barbecue grill to brown off and seal in the flavour. Squeeze half a lemon over the goat meat.

Place tomatoes in a roasting dish. Add celery and coriander.

Place goat into roasting dish – you want to make sure that once goat, tomatoes, and celery are in the dish, they almost fill it – like they're taking a relaxing bath!

Pour the canned tomatoes and red wine over the meat, then add stock. When all this is in the dish, the level of liquid should come up to about halfway up the sides. If not – add water until desired mark is reached.

Quarter the remaining lemon and add to dish.

Bake in the oven for 2.5 hours.

Take out of oven and serve with wild rice.

PORK BELLY

I've said it before, but I'll say it again – pork belly can be used in a variety of ways to create uniquely amazing flavours. This is a great way to prepare and cook it to have as a main meat dish – or you can chop it up and add to salads or pasta, just about anything.

1 Tbsp **olive oil**

Salt and **pepper**

600g **pork belly**

1 tsp **sesame oil**

2–3 Tbsp **Sweet Chilli Sauce** (see page 64)

Sprigs of **fresh thyme**

Sprigs of **fresh sage**

1 **red onion** – cut into rings

10g **ginger** – coarsely chopped

Preheat oven to 160°C.

Rub olive oil, salt and pepper into both sides of the pork belly. Rub sesame oil into the skin or fatty side. Pour sweet chilli sauce over.

Place thyme and sage in an ovenproof dish and place pork on top. Top with a couple of sage leaves, onion rings and ginger. Sprinkle with salt and pepper.

Roast in oven for 2.5 hours.

Take out and leave to sit for a further 10 minutes, then serve.

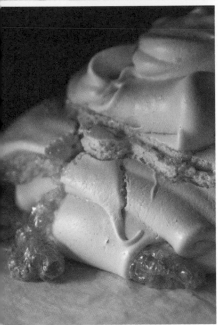

SWEET THINGS

Even though I cut out sugars for a year, there's certainly nothing wrong with the right kind of sugars every once in a while – everything in moderation as long as it's fresh! Good sugars, or natural sugars – real maple syrup, honey, pineapple, all fruits in fact – are awesome. Natural sugars also have other great benefits such as vitamins and antibacterial properties. Maple syrup has calcium, iron, magnesium, phosphorus, sodium, potassium, and zinc, plus vitamins such as thiamin, riboflavin, niacin, and B6 in it! How amazing is that?

STEPH'S PAVLOVA WITH CARAMELISED RHUBARB

Pavlova – it's like eating sugared clouds. Every time I make a pav it reminds me of my mum, Shirley, bless her. She really makes the best pavs – but I think that's what everyone thinks of their mothers' pavs. My kids love mine, not sure if they'd say it was the best in the world, but they sure do love this recipe. Angelo made it his own by adding mascarpone to the cream, but everything else is just pure classic Kiwi pavlova. – Steph

3 **egg whites**

1 cup **caster sugar**

½ tsp **vanilla essence**

½ tsp **white vinegar**

1 tsp **arrowroot**

65g **butter**

350g **rhubarb** – cut into 5 inch lengths

1 Tbsp **soft brown sugar** or **coconut sugar**

½ cup **warm water**

300ml **cream**

100g **mascarpone**

1 Tbsp **icing sugar**

1 whole **vanilla pod** – with seeds

½ tsp **vanilla essence**

TO SERVE

Blackberries

Icing sugar

Preheat oven to 120°C.

Beat eggs whites until stiff peaks form. While still beating, add sugar ¼ cup at a time.

Add vanilla essence, white vinegar and arrowroot as you mix. Continue beating at full speed for another 2 minutes.

Line a baking tray with baking paper and pour mixture onto paper. Mould into a low, rounded pyramid shape.

Place in oven for 1 hour. At end of cooking time, turn oven off, do NOT open the oven door! Leave to 'set' for 2–3 hours.

Meanwhile, melt butter in a pan over medium heat. Add rhubarb to butter and then add soft brown sugar or coconut sugar. Add warm water. Simmer mixture until the rhubarb breaks down and the liquid thickens, like a toffee. Leave to cool.

Whisk cream in a bowl. Add mascarpone, icing sugar and vanilla pod essence and seeds.

Once the pavlova is cool, carefully remove the top, or lid. Scoop half the cream mixture into the centre of the pavlova. Add the rhubarb mixture. Add more cream. Add blackberries. Then place the top or lid back on and dust with icing sugar.

Stand back...

TIP –Egg white mixture should be thick and marshmallow-y.

BREAD & BUTTER PUDDING

When we ran out of these at my café and deli, customers would actually get rather irate – and even say very bad words! Enough said…

And even though it's a bit cheeky calling it bread and butter, when there's no butter in it – it still tastes as good, if not better, than the good old traditional dish.

5 **eggs**

1 tsp **vanilla essence**

600ml **cream**

1 tsp **cinnamon**

¾ cup **sugar**

French stick or **croissants** – chopped into small pieces (equivalent to 1 standard loaf of bread)

1 cup **dates** – chopped.

1 cup **sultanas**

½ cup **blueberries**

½ cup **milk chocolate chips**

1 cup **coconut thread**

½ cup **pistachios** – roasted, unsalted

TOPPING

½ tsp **cinnamon**

1 tsp **sugar**

TO SERVE

Cream, **yoghurt** or **custard**

Preheat oven to 160°C. Grease 10–12 Texas muffin pans with butter.

Place eggs, vanilla essence, cream, and cinnamon in a bowl and whisk together. Add sugar. Whisk for 1 minute. Transfer into a jug for pouring.

Chop up bread or croissant into 2.5cm pieces. Place in a large bowl. Add dates, sultanas, blueberries, chocolate chips, coconut thread and pistachios. Mix together with hands place handfuls of the mixture into muffin tins. Make sure there are bits of bread at the bottom of the tins to soak up the good stuff. Press mixture into tins gently.

Slowly pour liquid mixture over the bread mixture in tins. Fill to three-quarter level.

Mix cinnamon and sugar together and sprinkle over the top of the pudding mixture.

Bake in oven for 15–20 minutes.

Serve with cream, yoghurt or custard and look out if you run out! You know what, better make it a double batch.

TIP – You can use any day-to-two-day-old bread – croissants, brioche, ciabatta, french stick – whatever adds up to about a loaf. Pre-soak your sultanas in brandy, and the dates in orange juice to make them plump, juicy and zesty.

LIME, ALMOND & COCONUT TEACAKES

There's nothing like a little bit of guilt-free sweet on a Sunday afternoon with friends. And the kids should really be allowed to have some too! The lime and coconut flavours just make me want to sing… "you put the lime in the coconut and drink it all up…"

500ml **water**

3 **limes** – stalks removed

100ml **water**

300g **coconut sugar**

½ tsp **cinnamon**

100g **butter** – softened

100g **GF self-raising flour**

100g **coconut flour**

100g **almond meal**

2 Tbsp **shredded coconut**

ICING

¾ cup **icing sugar**

Zest of 1 **lime**

2 Tbsp **coconut yoghurt**

75g **butter** – melted

Preheat oven to 170°C.

Place 500ml water in a small saucepan, add limes and bring to the boil. Lower the heat and simmer for 45 minutes – then let cool.

Once limes are cooked you should end up with 150ml of reduced lime syrup. Add to blender and blend. Add 100ml water and, blend. Add sugar and cinnamon and blend. Add butter and blend.

Place mixture in a big bowl. Add flours, almond meal and shredded coconut. Mix with a spoon until everything is combined.

Line six muffin pan with baking paper.

Divide mixture between muffin pans. Bake for 20 minutes.

TIP – Use a clean bottle to push the paper into each pan. Spray with oil spray or add a bit of butter and then spoon mixture into each tin.

ICING

Whisk together icing sugar, zest and coconut yoghurt in a bowl. Pour melted butter in and whisk. Set aside in a cool area for approximately 5 minutes or until the icing has thickened/stabilised.

Once the teacakes are cool, spread the icing over and decorate with whatever you feel like! Let the kids help out with that one. Yum!

ORANGE, CRYSTALLISED GINGER & DATE GF SCONES

Another awesome gluten-free recipe with a twist on an old favourite. Originating in Scotland around about 1500, the humble scone sure has been played with as a recipe, but the reasonwe love them is still the same — they make a good, hearty, filling, scrumptious snack or part of a meal. In New Zealand, scones have been dished up to thousands of hungry farmers for morning tea for years. If a scone can keep a Kiwi farmer going, what will they do for your kids!

2 cups **GF self-raising flour**

¼ cup **coconut sugar**

75g **butter**

¾ cup **orange juice** (freshly squeezed is always best!)

1 cup whole pitted **dates**

175ml **buttermilk**

½ cup **crystallised ginger**

Orange zest

Preheat oven to 170°C.

Place flour and sugar in a large bowl. Mix butter into flour by 'rubbing' with your fingers until the mixture looks like fine breadcrumbs.

Warm orange juice, dates and buttermilk in a small saucepan over medium heat and let curdle.

Pour buttermilk mixture into the flour mixture and mix through. Add crystallised ginger pieces and mix through.

Place baking paper on baking tray. Separate the dough into 5 roughly equal portions and place on tray.

Place orange zest on top and bake for 15 minutes.

Serve with fresh butter and marmalade or just eat them naked!

RASPBERRY TIRAMISU

The kids and I hang out all year for fresh raspberries. Where we live in the Cardrona Valley they tend not to grow wild, but there's a raspberry farm just down the road. I have to ban the kids from the kitchen if there's fresh raspberries in the fridge – before you know it, they're gone! Raspberries are amazing in any kind of dish – sweet or savoury. Their gorgeous tartness cuts through the sweet and fatty flavours of cheeses and cream, leaving the palette feeling revived and refreshed. They're also so good for you and full of antioxidants. This is a magic dish to serve for friends.

MASCARPONE CUSTARD MIXTURE

1 **egg yolk**

¼ cup **caster sugar**

¼ **vanilla pod** or 2 drops **vanilla essence**

90g **mascarpone cheese**

COFFEE MIXTURE

200ml **coffee** (ideally Fairtrade freshly ground espresso coffee, but plunger works well too)

1 Tbsp **caster sugar**

40ml **marsala**

2 drops of **vanilla essence**

TO ASSEMBLE

Savoiardi or **ladyfinger biscuits**

About 20 **raspberries**

Grated **dark chocolate**

1 Tbsp **raw cacao powder** or **cocoa powder**

Whisk the egg yolk and caster sugar together in a bowl until you get a soft buttery consistency.

Scrape seeds from the vanilla pod and add to egg mixture. Add the mascarpone cheese and mix through until it reaches a runny custard consistency.

Dissolve caster sugar into coffee and add marsala and vanilla essence.

Take 2 x 200ml glasses or vessels and start layering ingredients starting with the biscuits.

Cut the biscuits to size for the vessel or glass. Dunk the biscuits into coffee mixture and then place in the bottom of glass/vessel.

Cover soaked biscuits with mascarpone custard mixture. Add a layer of 5 raspberries. Then a layer of grated chocolate. Repeat layers – soaked biscuits, custard mixture, raspberries – then top with a final dusting of cacao or cocoa powder.

Chill in fridge for up to 2 hours then serve.

TIP – When you soak the biscuits don't over soak because they'll get all mushy and you don't want mushy biscuits. Oh, and don't under soak them as then they'll be too crunchy. It's a fine line between crunch and mush, but you'll know what I mean when you check them!

COCONUT VANILLA CUSTARD

Amazingly simple but delectably yummy, this is a super custard that everyone can enjoy. Eating dairy free, gluten free and vegetarian or vegan doesn't mean you can't enjoy a sweet treat every now and then and this custard is perfect! Eat it on its own or create your own fresh fruit masterpiece!

6 **egg yolks**

½ **vanilla pod** or 1 tsp **vanilla essence**

½ cup **coconut sugar**

400ml **coconut cream**

1 Tbsp **arrowroot** or **cornflour**

3 Tbsp **water**

Place egg yolks in a medium-sized saucepan. Scrape the seeds out from the vanilla pod and add to the yolks. Whisk.

Place pan over medium heat and continue whisking. Add coconut sugar to egg mixture. Add coconut cream gradually and continue whisking until it begins to simmer.

Mix arrowroot with water then add to the custard mix.

Continue to whisk until the mixture thickens.

Serve hot over fresh or preserved fruits or allow to cool and serve as a cold pudding.

TIP – Don't throw away the egg white use for a meringue or pavlova.

30 min   30 min   Serves 4   V

APPLE & CRANBERRY STRUDEL

Ok, strudel is definitely not Italian, Greek or Kiwi, but a good strudel is good for soul, as any Austrian will attest to! Around here in autumn we're so lucky to have access to an abundance of wild fruit trees, including heaps of apples and walnuts. If you know where to look, wild apples are the best as thy have retained their natural flavours without any genetic tampering.

FRUIT FILLING

½ cup **water**

4 cooking **apples** – peel, core and slice apples into ⅛ (granny smiths, braeburn and rose apples work well too)

Juice of ¼ a **lemon**

Zest of ½ a **lemon**

½ cup **coconut sugar**

½ **vanilla pod** or 1 tsp **vanilla essence**

½ cup **dried cranberries**

½ tsp **ground cardamon**

½ tsp **ground ginger**

½ tsp **cinnamon**

¾ cup **walnuts** – shelled and halved

1 Tbsp **maple syrup**

12 sheets **filo pastry**

TOPPING

Melted **butter**

Sliced **almonds**

½ tsp **coconut sugar**

¼ tsp **cinnamon**

TO SERVE

Icing sugar

Freshly **whipped cream**, **yoghurt** or **Coconut Vanilla Custard** (see page 166)

Preheat the oven to 175°C.

Place water, apples, lemon juice and zest and coconut sugar in a medium saucepan and bring to boil, cover then simmer for 5 minutes.

Scrape seeds from vanilla pod and add to the mix. Add dried cranberries, cardamom, ginger, and cinnamon and mix through. Set aside.

Place walnuts in a small frying pan over a medium heat. Add maple syrup and stir to make sure it coats and caramelises the walnuts, then take off the heat and place aside.

Place baking paper onto a flat baking tray. Lay out sheets of filo pastry onto tray. Add apple mixture to the middle of the pastry (like you're making a sausage roll) and place walnuts on top of fruit mixture. Roll up pastry like a big cigar and then trim off the ends.

Brush pastry roll with melted butter. Sprinkle with sliced almonds. Mix coconut sugar and cinnamon together and then sprinkle over the top of the almonds.

Bake in oven for 15–20 minutes or until golden.

Dust with icing sugar and serve with freshly whipped cream, yoghurt or my coconut vanilla custard.

LUCA'S GARDEN AND TERRARIUMS

I love to grow things. At my school in Wanaka we conducted a competition to see who could grow the biggest bean. I won – the rest is history! No, just kidding, but I did win and this really started my passion for growing things and seeing what I could get plants to do.

At 12 years old I realised I had a green thumb, I loved working with my plants, and I planted a vege garden. I asked for a tiny bit of land to grow some rhubarb, kale, spinach, tomatoes, and courgette. Mum said yes, and it went so well she gave me even more space for my patch. Dad and I built three big patches together – yes, I helped! Dad even let me take a couple of days off school to help him build the vege patches as learning about food and where it comes from is just as important to me and my family as learning your ABCs!

After about three months of having a pretty amazing vege garden, I discovered terrariums. They are so intricate and amazing and are their own whole little world and ecosystem. You can be so creative and make your terrarium a piece of art. My next idea is to grow an underwater terrarium, and I might be able to grow herbs like basil in it! Watch this little space!

Luca

FOR THE KIDS

It's the second most natural instinct we have after breathing. To eat. If you've ever seen a newborn baby, or animal for that matter, after they take a breath, the very next thing they do is start looking for food. So why not just keep that interest going? Fresh, homemade pumpkin purée straight from the garden to your little fella's bowl. There's no better way to foster a great relationship with food than with healthy, fresh, yummy homemade meals from the day they start on solids.

As they get older it'll be easy to keep them enthralled. Let them get their little fingers in dough, in the mixture, in the salad. Help them grate cheese, let them sniff lemons, garlic, let them taste everything. Nurturing a healthy fascination with good food is pretty easy if you start them young.

And don't feel you're denying them treats! When was the last time you scoffed a platter of fresh pineapple and oranges? Sweeter and more delicious than any horrid, plastic, sugar-coated jelly rubbish!

Remember, kids will do what you do. If you happily chomp your way through a salad foraged from your own garden, they will delightfully follow your lead. Especially if they had a hand in the gardening! Kids and vege gardens go together like peas and carrots! Get them gardening from the time they can hold a trowel and they'll eat whatever they've produced, prouder than Jack and his beanstalk.

LUCA'S ROAST TOMATO SOUP

I love this soup because it's so simple and tasty and I can make it myself – plus – they're MY tomatoes!

2kg **tomatoes**

30g **garlic** – peeled

3 Tbsp **extra virgin olive oil**

800ml **chicken** or **vegetable stock**

Handful of **basil**

Salt and **pepper**

TO SERVE

Parmesan cheese

Fresh basil

Preheat oven to 200°C.

Place tomatoes in an ovenproof saucepan, top with garlic bulb, drizzle with olive oil and roast for 25–35 minutes or until the tomatoes have browned and softened and liquid has released.

Put the saucepan on the stove and add stock, basil and salt and pepper to taste then simmer for 35 minutes. Take off stove and blend with stick blender until smooth.

Serve with Parmesan and fresh basil.

45 min   45 min    Serves 4–6   ⊗ GF   ⊗ NF

LUCIA'S RABBIT PIE

Rabbit Pie is my favourite pie in the world – because my Dad makes it. It has a special touch, but I can't tell you what it is – that's a family secret! I have tried shooting my own rabbit for the pie, but I'm better with a bow and arrows and rabbits are too fast for me to get with my bow yet. I love this pie because rabbit is really tasty and the vegetables make it so yummy.

FILLING

1½L **water**

1 tsp **salt**

600g **rabbit meat** off the bone

120g **butter**

2 cloves **garlic**

½ **leek** – sliced

1 Tbsp **coconut sugar**

1 Tbsp **wholegrain mustard**

100g **streaky bacon**

180g sliced **white mushrooms**

20g **fresh thyme**

Salt and **pepper**

250ml **coconut cream** or **cream**

2 medium **carrots**

1 cup **chicken** or **rabbit stock**

2 Tbsp **arrowroot** or **cornflour**

60g **powdered Parmesan cheese**

PASTRY

100g **GF flour**

75g **almond flour**

75g **coconut flour**

125g **unsalted butter**

2 **eggs** – 1 chilled, 1 separated and white discarded

1 Tbsp **cold water**

1 tsp **cumin seeds**

FILLING

Place water, salt and rabbit meat in a medium-sized saucepan. Boil for 30 minutes until meat is tender. Set aside.

Place butter, garlic, leek, coconut sugar and wholegrain mustard in a large saucepan and cook until golden. Add bacon and rabbit meat and cook for a few minutes until bacon is soft and golden.

Add the mushrooms, thyme, salt and pepper, and stir-fry for a few minutes, then add coconut cream or cream, carrots and stock and cook for 10 minutes. Mix the arrowroot into ½ cup of cold water, stir until lump-free, then add to the rabbit mixture. Stir through until thickened.

Take off the heat and stir through the Parmesan. Set aside to cool while you make the pastry.

PASTRY

Preheat oven to 180°C.

Combine the flours in a bowl. Add the butter. Using your fingertips, rub the butter into the flours until you've made a coarse dough.

Whisk whole egg and the water in a bowl. Add to the dough. Use a fork to blend the egg and water into the dough mixture until a consistent texture is achieved. Add the caraway seeds and mix together. Wrap dough in plastic wrap and chill for 15 minutes.

Roll dough out on a floured surface or greaseproof paper. Use to line a pre-greased pie dish, making sure you have enough dough left over to roll out for the top. Now it's time for the filling! Hooray! Pour in then place the rolled-out top on and seal with the egg yolk.

Bake the pie in the oven for 25–30 minutes or until golden brown.

OSCAR'S BROWN TROUT

I love spending time with Dad, especially when we go fishing together. So it's not really about catching fish, it's about spending time together and having good talks with my Dad, but it's definitely a bonus. I love this trout recipe because it tastes smoky and moist. The best thing about fishing is just being relaxed and happy. And then there's the excitement of catching a fish! It feels so exciting when a fish is on the line, it's like I can't let go – like it's my destiny!

1 medium (800g) **fresh brown** or **rainbow trout**

1 Tbsp **Sweet Chilli Sauce** (see page 64)

Salt and **pepper**

Pinch of **smoked paprika**

5g **fresh ginger** – chopped

1 Tbsp **fresh mint leaves** – chopped

Prepare the trout – clean and pat dry, removing any loose scales. Butterfly the trout, slicing cleanly down the middle of the belly, spread open.

Rub sweet chilli sauce, then sprinkle salt and pepper, all over.

Add the smoked paprika, ginger and fresh mint and rub over fish.

Put into a smoker – or if you don't have a smoker, wrap in tinfoil, and place on the barbecue. Or you can place in the oven on 180°C. For all cooking methods, cook for around 15 minutes, turning as it cooks.

DELICIOUS!

Best served with your choice of salads from the greens section or a handful of fresh watercress with a drizzle of olive oil, lemon juice and seasoning.

INDEX

CHEERS

This second book would never have been possible without the support and amazing generosity of some truly amazing people and companies. Honestly, team, I am the luckiest guy in the world to have such an incredible team of people behind me every step of the way. This book is a bit different to *The Game Chef*, but you guys have been there, trusting my dream, believing in my vision, and keeping me from losing my head when it all got pretty full on! For all of this, and for getting the Wild Kitchen philosophy and how important it is to me and to my family... cheers!

To the entire Beatnik team for their enduring support and belief in this book and whole concept of Wild living and eating. You guys are amazing – and I never, ever thought a book could be put together so fast! Sally, you're incredible, mate – and I'm just blown away by how you do what you do. Sally took almost all the photos guys – isn't she awesome! And speaking of awesome – Martin – you're the best! Cheers brother!

Again, to Carla Munro, for the words. I don't know how you do it, but you write exactly what's in my head without me even having to say it. It's like you have a direct line into my wild brain! Haha, but seriously, thanks, love. You're a brilliant writer and a great friend.

As always, a hunter without a big chunk of land needs the support from high country stations, and in this book, I owe a huge thanks to Guy and Davida (Dee) Mead and Tim and Nicky from Dingleburn Station. Also to Willy and Sarah Scurr from Cardrona – mate, your lands in the Cardrona Valley are just epic. Thanks so much for being the best neighbour in the world.

And actually, to the whole Cardrona Valley community – Cardrona Hotel, Cardrona Alpine Resort, and the rest of the entire valley. So glad to be part of this awesome village.

And to Backcountry Saddle Expeditions, Deb and Rosie and my mate Smokey the horse, cheers for teaching me to ride so I can bow hunt from the saddle!

Speaking of community – Dean, from New World Wanaka, mate, you're the best. Thank you so much – as always. You consistently encourage my confidence in local supermarkets – you're doing a great job!

Daniel from TyreLAND Wanaka – those wheels on the 4x4 go round and round – thanks to you!

To the fishing experts, Maven Fishing, CTS Fishing and Swift Fly Fishing Company – you guys sure do know fishing in New Zealand!

Kiwi Outdoor Oven Company – what an unbelievable honour to have one of your very own pizza ovens in my backyard. Friday nights will never be the same!

Hunters Element – no one should ever hunt in New Zealand without your gear!

Paul Brian from Lineside Automotive and Cruisers... man, what can I say, and thanks so much for the Super Mini Booster Battery Pack! Man, hope I never need to use it – but better safe than sorry in the places I go!

To the awesome team at Cactus Outdoor, I'm a total convert! Love the gear, love your attitude, and love what you're doing.

Barbara Poots – darling, again, your platters have meant the world. I don't think people understand, it's not just presentation, it's the whole package – the aroma of beautiful food on wine-soaked oak staves – so amazing.

Mike and Linda at Attitude Archery, thanks so very much! I mean it. You know how much I love my bows!

Kilwell Sports NZ – brilliant. Just brilliant.

Coopers Tyres for keeping me on the road in the Wild Kitchen truck – it's a beauty and deserved the best tyres around! Cheers team!

And because she's a bloody beauty of a truck, she deserves the best accessories a man or woman can buy – and you guys have them! Thanks so much ARB 4X4 Accessories New Zealand!

Huge thanks to Yamaha NZ, both Yamaha Marine and Yamaha Motor.

To Brendon Frew from FREWZA Boats in Invercargill – cannot wait for this wee project to be finished mate! Good on ya!

I want to say a special thanks always to Jon and Bailey from Pango Productions for believing in me and my story.

To Levi Harrell, mate, thanks for coming with me on adventures and taking some pretty epic shots. Love having a great guy with a camera to shoot what I shoot!

To my beautiful, incredible kids. This one really is for you guys, you know that. You guys make my day every day. The fact that I have you in my life is just so precious to me and I am so damn proud of every one of you.

Luca, you're a young man with so much heart, so much get-up-and-go, so much creativity, I just can't even express how amazing you are. I love how you've taken to gardening and your terrariums and plants with such a passion – it just blows me away.

Oscar, my little man. Your smile lights up the world my man. Your energy, your humour, just gets me. I love taking you hunting and fishing, knowing you'll love it as much as I do. You're a champion and I am so proud of you.

Lucia, my daughter, my darling girl, you kick butt baby! I feel like I never have to worry about you, because you're so vivacious, so amazing, and so strong! I LOVE that you love your bow and that you're a bloody great shot! I love that you love all sports and you're good at all of them! I love that you're who you are and that you are my girl. Keep kicking it baby girl!

Steph, darling Steph. Thank you my love. Thank you with all my heart. For believing in me and this journey, for putting up with this vision of mine, and not just putting up with it, you've taken it as your own. I couldn't do what I do without your support. I couldn't be who I am today without you. You are my wife. My love. My conscience. You are my everything, really. Love you. xxx

Angelo